MOON AND SUN

ماه و خورشید

برگزیده‌ای از رباعیات

مولانا جلال الدین رومی

برگردان:
زارا هوشمند

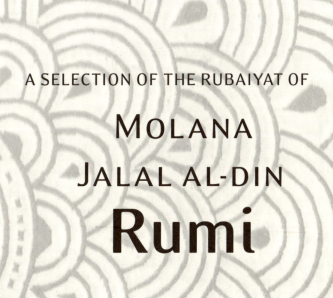

A SELECTION OF THE RUBAIYAT OF

Molana
Jalal al-din
Rumi

TRANSLATION
Zara Houshmand

Copyright © 2020 by Zara Houshmand

All rights reserved.

Published in the United States by Amrevan Books.

Printed in Malaysia by Imago.

www.amrevanbooks.com

Hardback ISBN: 978-1-7344225-0-4

First Edition

Book design by Kathleen Burch

Contents

Introduction · 7

Love's Lightning · 13

Secrets, Speech, and Silence · 23

The Heart's Messenger · 33

Show Your Face · 43

Wrestling with the Angel · 57

Die for Love · 75

Drunk on the Essence · 89

Alone in the Desert · 103

Reunion · 115

In the Garden · 125

The Wisdom of Insanity · 137

Passing Shadows · 149

Burning in the Flame · 159

The Open Embrace · 171

Moonlight Brings, Moonlight Takes Away · 185

Endnotes · 201

Acknowledgments · 204

Introduction

THESE RUBAIYAT, OR QUATRAINS, were composed by Jalal al-Din Mohammad Balkhi, known as Rumi, a thirteenth century Muslim theologian and Sufi mystic, and one of the greatest poets of the Persian language. They are a selection from almost two thousand such quatrains that, along with many longer ghazals, comprise the DIVAN-E SHAMS. These poems poured out during a period of Rumi's life when he was intensely affected by his relationship with his spiritual mentor and soulmate, Shams al-Din Tabrizi.

Legend describes Shams — whose name means "sun" — as a wandering dervish, unschooled, an ugly man but charismatic. His own words, only recently made accessible in English, present a much subtler picture. He was an accomplished scholar who hid his learning, an iconoclast, and a fearsome enemy of all hypocrisy. He traveled widely in search of the great spiritual teachers of his time, but kept his distance from the dervish schools that would normally have accommodated such a traveler. He refused to beg, and instead earned a meager living at temporary jobs as he traveled.

His relationship with Rumi also defied categories, blurring the traditional roles of master and disciple. Rumi held the belief that at any one time, a single saint living in the world serves as an AXIS MUNDI, a center around which all spiritual energy revolves. He believed that in Shams he had found this saint. It is clear from Shams's own teachings that he likewise saw Rumi as a saint, though one who had something to learn from him.

The synergy of their friendship was a mutually fueled fire of the spirit.

The DIVAN-E SHAMS is unusual in that its title, which means THE COLLECTED POEMS OF SHAMS, would normally indicate that Shams is the author. Rumi may have chosen such a self-effacing title to honor Shams, but he may also be implying that the poems arise from Shams's voice speaking through Rumi, as the sun's light is reflected by the moon.

Tradition also contributes to confusion over the true authorship of many of these poems. Some poems popularly attributed to Rumi were in fact written by earlier writers. Other poems now attributed to Rumi were not included in the earliest collections of his writing but were added a century later. Oral transmission plays a role in the confusion. Even when composed on paper, poems would often be memorized and passed on orally. Poems by earlier writers may have been included in the collection simply because Rumi recited them on occasion, and the original author was forgotten. It remains possible that some of these poems were actually composed by Shams.[1]

Rumi was often described as improvising poetry spontaneously in the midst of the meditative whirling dance that was central to his practice. Although it is delightful to imagine poems birthed in the exuberance of an ecstatic ritual, these verses also conform skillfully to literary convention and are masterful exemplars of their kind.

The RUBAI, or quatrain (the plural is RUBAIYAT), is one of the oldest verse forms in Persian and has an unusually flexible meter. Examples of pre-Islamic rubaiyat expressing Zoroastrian aphorisms have survived, and it is also the oldest verse form used for the expression of Sufi thought in Persian. A RUBAI typically begins with an epigrammatic couplet, often opening with a provocative, attention-grabbing line. The thought pivots in the third, unrhymed line, serving as a bridge to the final resolution, which rhymes with the first couplet. Many poems repeat the same word or phrase after the rhyme word, creating an effect that may be as strong as a refrain or as light as a feminine rhyme.

Rumi's poetry is exceptionally musical even by the standards of Persian verse. For example, he embellishes the typical AABA rhyme scheme with much internal rhyme that is not strictly required by the form. In these translations, I have not tried to duplicate the original meter or rhyme, but only to honor the musical quality of the original.

THAT RUMI CHOSE THE LANGUAGE of romantic love to address a vast body of poetry to his spiritual guide is explained by the confluence of Persian literary tradition and the ecstatically devotional, mystical path that Rumi and Shams traveled together. This coupling of romantic language with spiritual intent is seen also in the medieval European troubadour lyrics and the literature of courtly love. There is evidence suggesting that these themes originated in the East, and reached Western writers through the traffic of the Crusades.

One of the most difficult problems that arises in translating the original poetry is the use of ungendered pronouns in Persian. The pronoun oo can be rendered equally as "he," "she," "it," or even "God," depending on context. The ambiguity inherent in the language allows for multiple interpretations, and such meaningful ambiguity is a much prized quality in Persian poetry. In English, however, one is forced to choose. I have generally chosen the feminine pronoun where details suggest the image of a woman, or where the physical beauty of the beloved is emphasized, and varied the choices elsewhere as a reminder to the reader that there is more here than meets the eye.

Many of the masks that the lover assumes are shaped by convention rather than biography. When Rumi portrays himself as a wasted drunkard, or insane, he is drawing not on literal fact but on literary archetypes that were commonly used and yet deeply felt as true embodiments of the ideas and emotions being expressed. Rumi's genius lies in his ability to inhabit such roles with both utter sincerity and playful skill as he conveys his very direct and deceptively simple reports of the heart's struggle.

ZARA HOUSHMAND

Love's Lightning

برق عشق

ON A LATE AUTUMN DAY IN 1244, Jalal al-Din Rumi stopped with a group of friends at an inn in Konya. There, a stranger recognized him — not surprising, considering that Rumi was a highly respected scholar of theology who often preached at the mosque. The old man observed Rumi intently. Finally, he approached and asked a question.

The question had roots in a longstanding debate, and it was subtle yet penetrating, turning on whether ecstatic mystical experience placed one above the laws set by the prophet Mohammad's example. Here its intent was direct: a test of an eminent teacher's faith, understanding, and integrity.

The old man was Shams al-Din Tabrizi, a Sufi of extraordinary spiritual and intellectual accomplishments. He was a seeker, unattached to any school or sect, who traveled incognito in search of holy men, and earned a humble living on his way by weaving or tutoring children. For years Shams had sought a companion with the spiritual maturity to share his experience, someone worthy of his complete trust. Now he was found.

Shams later described a sweetness and radiant purity of spirit that shone in their brief exchange. It was a transcendent moment of recognition and sheer presence — love at first sight.

Rumi brought Shams to his home to continue their discussion, and from that day on, the two men were bound together in a friendship that was all-consuming.

Your love stirs the ocean into reckless storms.
At your feet, the clouds drop their pearls.
Dark smoke rises in the sky, a fire burns
Where your love's lightning strikes the earth.

از عشق تو دریا بہ همه شور انگیزد   در پای تو ابرها درّ می ریزد

از عشق تو برقی به زمین افتاده ست   این دود به آسمان از آن می خیزد

You're the road of love, and at the end, my home,
One of the crowd and yet I see you crowned.
I see you in the stars, in the sun and moon,
Here in the green leaves, and high on the throne.

هم منزل عشق و هم رهت می بینم   در بنده و در مروّهت می بینم

در اختر و خورشید و مهت می بینم   در برگ و گیاه و در گهت می بینم

Love is what gives joy to all creation.
Love is what does justice to joy.
I was born of Mother Love in the beginning.
To that mother, endless praise and blessing.

عشق آن باشد که خلق را دارد شاد   عشق آن باشد که داد شادی ها داد

زاده است مرا مادر عشق از اول   صد رحمت و آفرین بر آن مادر باد

My heart is your student; it studies love,
And, like the night, it kneels before the day.
Like oil, it flows to the flame it feeds:
Wherever I turn, love burns before me.

شاگرد توست دل که عشق آموز است   مانندۀ شب که رفته پای روز است

هر جا که روم صورت عشق است به پیش   زیرا روغن در پی روغن سوز است

My heart boils up, aspiring to your heat,
Closes its eyes to grope what you see clear,
Drinks poison, thirsting for your antidote,
Forges itself as a ring to grace your ear.

می جوشد دل که تا به جوش تو رسد / بی هوش شده است تا به هوش تو رسد

می نوشد زهر تا به نوش تو رسد / چون حلقه شده است تا به گوش تو رسد

I'm so close to you that I'm far apart,
So completely merged that I'm separate,
So vastly exposed that I'm concealed,
So whole and sound that I'll never be healed.

از بس که به نزدیک توام من دورم / وز غایت آمیزش تو مهجورم

وز کثرت پیدا شدگی مستورم / وز صحت بسیار چنین رنجورم

So far and high did my heart's bird fly
That worlds upon worlds opened secrets up.
So many ways he encompassed the sky
That world and beyond are a drop in his cup.

مرغ دل من ز بس که پرواز آورد   عالم عالم جهان جهان راز آورد
چندان به همه سوی جهان بیرون شد   کاین هر دو جهان به قطره ای باز آورد

If you don't heed my call and answer me
With joy, with the wine of your words, who will?
Shepherd of the world, refuge of the soul,
If you don't keep me from the wolf, who will?

گر تو نکنی سلام ما را درپی   چون حمله نشاطی و سلامی چون می
چوپان جهانی و امان جان ها   دفع گرگ گر نکنی هی، هی، هی

Don't walk away, I'll pay your price!
Look here! I'm the light you see by.
Come work with me, your deeds will shine!
Don't quit now – I'm your marketplace!

مگریز از من که من خریدار توام   در من بنگر که نور دیدار توام

در کار من آ که رونق کار توام   بیزار مشو ز من که بازار توام

If sadness ruled from here to the horizon,
He would not be sad who holds love firm.
If love makes even one atom dance,
That atom holds all this world and the next.

گر جمله آفاق همه غم بگرفت   بی غم بود آن که عشق محکم بگرفت

یک ذره نگر که پای در عشق بکوفت   و آن ذره جهان شد که دو عالم بگرفت

It is treasure buried in earth, concealed —
Both from the pious and faithless, concealed.
We saw that it surely was love, concealed —
This hidden thing left us naked, revealed.

گنجیست نهاده در زمین پوشیده   از ملت کفر و اهل دین پوشیده

دیدیم که عشق است یقین پوشیده   گشتیم برهنه از چنین پوشیده

Secrets, Speech, and Silence

رازها، رمزها و ناگفته‌ها

TO THE DISMAY OF HIS FOLLOWERS, Rumi secluded himself with Shams, absorbed in conversation that continued for days and nights, even weeks on end. What they talked about remains wrapped in secrecy.

Shams wrote that his own initiation into the Sufi mysteries — symbolized by the bestowal of a ceremonial cloak — came not from any teacher alive, but from the Prophet Mohammad himself who appeared to him in a dream. It was not a cloak of cloth that would wear and tear, he said, but a cloak of SOHBAT — speech or conversation. It did not consist of words that could be understood by the intellect, but a spiritual exchange that is "not of yesterday, today or tomorrow."[2]

Rumi resorts to silence to express how knowledge of the ineffable is transmitted from one person to another. Just as other Persian poets use their pen-name in the conclusion of a ghazal, Rumi often closes his poems with the signature KHAMUSH, which means "be quiet" — a call to silence that echoes beyond his words to leave us reflecting on their deeper truth.

We speak another language, not this tongue.
There's another home apart from heaven and hell.
Free spirits draw life from another source –
That pure gem is mined from a different course.

جز دوزخ و فردوس مکانی دیگر است ما را به جز این زبان زبانی دگر است

آن گوهر پاکشان ز کانی دگر است آزاده دلان زنده به جان دگرند

Last night, discreetly, I asked the wise old man
To reveal to me the secret of the world.
He whispered softly, "You'll know by knowing,
Not what can be told. Now hush!"

کز من سخن از سرِ جهان هیچ مپوش با پیر خرد نهفته می‌گفتم دوش

کین دانستنی است، گفتنی نیست، خموش نرمک نرمک مرا همی گفت به گوش

A friend who feeds me pleasure and kindness
Sews me a robe of my own skin and veins.
My body's the cloak for my Sufi heart,
The world my house of worship, he my Lord.

پرورده ناز و نعمت آن دوست مرا   بردوخت مرقع از رگ و پوست مرا

تن خرقه و اندر او دل ماصوفی   عالم همه خانقاه و شیخ اوست مرا

Hide this mystery in your soul, and hide
Even from yourself, my spirit's state.
If you're alive, hide me like your soul —
Make my heresy the summit of your faith.

اسرار مرا نهانی اندر جان کن   احوال مرا ز خویش هم پنهان کن

گر جان داری مرا چو جان پنهان کن   وین کفر مرا پیشرو ایمان کن

I asked, "What should I do?" He said, "Just this —
Keep asking what to do." I said, "That's it?
Is that the best that you can do?" He turned to me,
"Truth seeker, stick to this: What should I do?"

گفتم چه کنم؟ گفت همین که چه کنم   گفتم به از این چاره ببین که چه کنم

رو کرد به من گفت که ای طالب دین   پیوسته بر این باش بر این که چه کنم

There's no way to explain this secret.
Nothing I could say of him is worthy.
Something within me holds happiness,
Yet there's no way to point a finger at it.

اسرار ز دست داده می توانم   و آن را بسر اگشاد می توانم

چیزیست درونم که مرا خوش دارد   انگشت بر او نهاد می توانم

I will not tell the secret my friend spoke,
I will not pierce that precious pearl.
I have not slept these many nights for fear
That I might spill those words out as I sleep.

سرّ سخن دوست نمی‌آرم گفت   درّیست گران بهانی آرم سفت
ترسم که به خواب درگویم سخنی   شب‌هاست که از بیم نمی‌آرم خفت

I paused for a while among the crowd,
But found no trace of loyalty among them.
It's best that I hide from the view of men,
Like the gleam in the iron, or fire within the flint.

یک چند میان خلق کردیم درنگ   زایشان به وفا نه بوی دیدیم نه رنگ
آن به که نهان شویم از دیده خلق   چون آب در آهن و چو آتش در سنگ

He is king who knows you, even cloaked.
He hears your cries, even though unmouthed.
Fine words always have something to sell.
He who knows silence is the one I serve.

شاهیست که تو هر چه بپوشی داند / بی کام و زبان گر بخروشی داند

هر کس هوس سخن فروشی داند / من بنده آنم که خموشی داند

My love kindly came to me last night.
I begged Night, "Keep our mystery from the light."
"On the contrary," Night said, "you hold the sun
Within you, how can I bring morning?"

دوش آمده بود از سر لطفی یارم / شب را گفتم فاش مکن اسرارم

شب گفت پس و پیش نگه کن آخر / خورشید تو داری، ز کجا صبح آرم؟

He who set my world on fire and made
A hundred tongues of flame consume my tongue –
When fire blazed around me on all sides,
I sighed, and he covered my mouth with his hand.

آنکس که بر آتش جهانم بنهاد   صد گونه زبانه بر زبانم بنهاد

چون شش جهتم شعله آتش بگرفت   آه کردم و دست بر دهانم بنهاد

Drunk, I asked my teacher, "Please, I need to know
What it means to be or not to be."
He answered me and said, "Go!
Relieve the suffering of the world and you'll be free."

استاد مرا بگفتم اندر مستی   کاگاه کن ز نیستی و هستی

او داد مرا جواب و گفتا که برو   گر رنج ز خلق دور داری رستی

The Heart's Messenger

پیام آور دل

IT IS SAID THAT WHEN Shams first appeared, Rumi's books went up in flames of spontaneous combustion. In another account of their first meeting, Shams tosses Rumi's books into a pool of water. Miraculously, the pages are undamaged. Only Rumi's attachment to them is ripped out, fluttering down in a moment of stunned realization.

As these stories suggest, Shams led Rumi beyond book learning and into the realm of Sufi practices that aim at transforming the heart and mind. Under his guidance, Rumi experienced a flowering of the heart that expressed itself in a prolific eruption of poetry. It was Shams too who taught Rumi the whirling dance that is a meditation in motion, and many of his poems flowed extemporaneously in the midst of the dance.

Although we think of poetry now as a matter for books and private perusal, in Persian culture, poetry has always been married to music and shared aloud, whether as entertainment or in a devotional setting. SAMA‘, the term that is used for the devotional dance, literally means "listening" and originally it referred to gatherings where poetry and music were heard.

When your love began to fill up my heart,
Whatever else I had was burnt away.
Logic and book-learning were tossed on the fire,
Now I study song and poetry all day.

تا در دل من عشق تو اندوخته شد   جز عشق تو هر چه داشتم سوخته شد
عقل و سبق و کتاب بر طاق نهاد   شعر و غزل و دوبیتی آموخته شد

If, in love's seminary, they debate
The line between love's state and its report,
Here no theologian's ruling abides.
On love, their eminences' tongues are tied.

در مدرسه عشق اگر قال بود   کی فرق میان قال با حال بود
در عشق ندادهیچ مفتی فتوی   در عشق زبان مفتیان لال بود

He stopped my cries, "Be silent!"
Then answered my silence, "Come shout!"
I swelled with sound, he demanded, "Be still!"
I was still, then he made me sing.

بخروشیدم، گفت خموشت خواهم	خاموش شدم، گفت خروشت خواهم
برجوشیدم، گفت که نی، ساکن باش	ساکن گشتم، گفت بجوشت خواهم

This body's molded clay is my heart's cup,
My well-aged thoughts are its new-pressed wine.
My heart sets a trap with these grains of truth —
I speak the words, but the message comes from my heart.

این شکل سفالین تنم جام دلست	و اندیشهٔ پخته‌ام می خام دلست
این دانهٔ دانش همگی دام دلست	این من گفتم ولیک پیغام دلست

There's another kind of calm in the congress of lovers,
A different oblivion in the wine of love.
The knowledge that the classroom yields is one thing,
And love — love is something else again.

در مجلس عشاق قراری دگر است   وین باده عشق را خماری دگر است
آن علم که در مدرسه حاصل کردند   کار دگر است و عشق کاری دگر است

Today, as ever, I'm wasted with wine.
Shut the mind's door, touch the bow to the string.
There are a hundred ways to pray, to kneel,
To bow at the shrine of my love's beauty.

امروز چو هر روز خرابیم خراب   مگشای در اندیشه و برگیر رباب
صد گونه نماز است رکوع است و سجود   آن را که جمال دوست باشد محراب

All my heart speaks, openly or hidden,
Concerns her musky hair, its scent that strays —
My heart is flustered by its wild ways,
And thus perturbed, flings words in disarray.

دل هر چه در آشکار و پنهان گوید زان موی چو مشک عنبر افشان گوید

این آشفته است و او پریشان دانم کاشفته سخن‌های پریشان گوید

Sit in my heart like a secret — don't go.
Rest on my head like a turban — don't go.
"I come and go," you say, "in the beat of a heart."
Don't tease me, cunning heart-thief — please don't go.

که در دل ما نشین چو اسرار و مرو که بر سر ما نشین چو دستار و مرو

گفتی که چو دل زود روم و زود آیم عشوه مده ای دلبر عیار و مرو

I'm not a poet. I don't earn my bread
By it, or flaunt my skill, or even think
My art, my talent, more than just a cup.
I only drink when my love hands it to me.

شاعر نیم وز شاعری نان نخورم   وز فضل نلافم و غم آن نخورم

فضل و هنرم یکی قدح می باشد   وان نیز مگر ز دست جانان نخورم

Where do you come from, cry of the bowed string,
Full of fire, revolt, and sedition?
You're a spy, the heart's desert envoy –
Its secrets are the message you sing.

ای بانک رباب از کجا می آیی   پر آتش و پر قتنه و پر غوغائی

جاسوس دلی و پیک آن صحرائی   اسرار دلست هر چه می فرمائی

Each part of me proclaims my love for her,
Each scrap of me, a tongue that speaks her name.
I'm the lute in her arms, the flute at her lips,
And my cries arise from her fingertips.

بر هر جزء من نشان معشوق منست   هر پارهٔ من زبان معشوق منست

چون چنگ منم در بر او تکیه زده   این ناله ام از بنان معشوق منست

That Turk who gladdens my heart with her smile,
Drives me to anguish with her flying hair.
She made me write the words that set her free,
And wrote the words that made a slave of me.

ترکی که دلم شاد کند خندهٔ او   دارد به غم زلف پراکندهٔ او

بستد ز من او خطی به آزادی خویش   آورد خطی که من شدم بندهٔ او

I wrote a poem that made my love angry.
"Do you measure me in couplets and rhyme?"
Why must you ruin whatever I build?
"What structure," said she, "could contain me?"

گفتم بیتی نگار از من رنجید یعنی که به وزن بیت ما را سنجید

گفتم که چه ویران کنی این بیت مرا گفتا به کدام بیت خواهم گنجید

The names I gave him — wine, sometimes the cup.
At times he was raw silver, gold, refined.
A tiny seed, at times my prey, my trap —
All this because I could not say his name.

که باده لقب نهادم و که جامش گاهی زر پخته گاه سیم خامش

که دانه گاه صید و گاهی دامش این جمله چراست تا نگویم نامش

Show Your Face

بنمای رخ

ALL DESIRE, ALL AESTHETIC PLEASURE, is a reaching for God in disguise. Without some taste of worldly love, how can we imagine divine love?

The notion that the physical beauty of the beloved bears witness to the perfection of God's creation has a long history in Persian poetry, and erotic ambiguity is an essential energy of this tradition. But Shams was sixty years old when he met Rumi, not an attractive youth by any stretch of the imagination.

What then lies behind the sublimely romantic poems that Rumi addresses to Shams? The presence of the spiritual friend and guide offers a glimpse of divine presence, and when the desire for this presence is honed to an intense longing, a single-minded obsession, it can spur us forward on the path. With bold playfulness and a supremely confident mastery of the tradition, Rumi reinvents the notion of romantic love as a mirror of divine love. How beautifully the finger pointing to the moon glows in the moonlight!

How could the soul that holds your image
Ever fade or decay? The crescent moon,
Though waning, thin and pale, begins its voyage
And grows to full perfection very soon.

جانی که در او از تو خیالی باشد   کی آن جان را نقل و زوالی باشد

مه در نقصان گر چه هلالی باشد   نقصان وی آغاز کمالی باشد

Happiness laughed till you clapped your hands.
The cup was passed, you tapped your toes.
From under the veil a brow rose, arched —
Your fingers snapped, you danced for that rainbow.

خندید فرح تا بزنی انگشتک   گردید قدح تا بزنی انگشتک

بنمودت ابروی خود از زیر نقاب   چون قوس قزح تا بزنی انگشتک

Seeking love, I see it winding in your curls.

Seeking life, I see it walking down your street.

Driven by deep thirst, I drink, only to see

A dream upon the water: you face to face with me.

گر دل طلبم در خم مویت بینم ور جان طلبم بر سر کویت بینم

از غایت تشنگی اگر آب خورم در آب همه خیال رویت بینم

My love is beautiful — one of her faults.

Delicate, tender — that's two and three.

But the real reason that people shun her?

Her flawless perfection is the sin they flee.

دلدار ظریف است و گناهش اینست زیبا و لطیف است و گناهش اینست

آخر به چه عیب می‌گریزند از او؟ از عیب عفیف است و گناهش اینست

The lovely one whispers under her breath,
And you go mad, witless, no reason left.
O Lord, what is this magic spell she casts
That plants itself in the stoniest heart?

دلدار بزیر لب بخواند چیزی   دیوانه شوی عقل نماند چیزی

یارب چه فسونست که او می خواند   کاندر دل سنگ می نشاند چیزی

A rare catch has come my way, what am I to do?
She's put my head in such a daze, what am I to do?
I'm a holy man on the path, a sham. When an idol
Gives a kiss like this, what am I to do?

افتاده مرا عجب شکاری چه کنم   و اندر سرم افکنده خماری چه کنم

سالوسم و زاهدم و لیکن در راه   گر بوسه دهد مرا نگاری چه کنم

She made my night more splendid than the day,
Made body subtle, more sublime than soul.
My lips sought hers, but their honey
Sweetly left no room for my kiss.

از روز شریف تر شد از وی شب من   وز روح لطیف تر شد این قالب من

رفت این لب من طالب او را بوسد   از شهد شکر نبود جای لب من

Look at her black hair, that graceful pose,
Imagine the sweetness of those lips.
"Alms, please!" I begged for a kiss.
She laughed, "Think what a profit you'd make!"

آن زلف سیاه و قد رعناش نگر   شیرینی آن لعل شکر خاش نگر

گفتم که زکات حسن یک بوسه بده   برگشت و بخنده گفت سوداش نگر

My delightful, duplicitous idol arrives
With a smile biting those two ruby lips!
Stealing my heart that day was not enough.
Today you're back, intent on my life.

خوش خوش صنما تازه رخان آمده ای   خندان به دو لب لعل گزان آمده ای

آن روز دلم ز سینه بردی بس نیست   کامروز دگر به قصد جان آمده ای

A perfect love, a heart-thief, a beauty —
My heart speaks and yet my tongue is mute.
It's rare, it's strange, it's a mystery —
Pure water flows beside me, yet I'm thirsty.

عشقی به کمال و دلربایی به جمال   دل بر سخن و زبان ز گفتن شده لال

زین نادره تر کجا بود هرگز حال   من تشنه و پیش من روان آب زلال

Your homeland was the heavens, but you thought
You belonged here in this world of dust.
In the dust you drew your portrait, but
You left out just one thing: your first, true place.

ای آنکه تو بر فلک وطن داشته‌ای   خود را از جهان خاک پنداشته‌ای

بر خاک تو نقش خویش بگذاشته‌ای   وان چیز که اصل توست بگذاشته‌ای

When your love is determined to spill my blood
My soul leaps from this cage of human clay.
He's a godless infidel who has the chance to taste
The sin of your sweet lips, and lives on, chaste.

عشق تو خوشی چو قصد خونریز کند   جان از قفس قالب من خیز کند

کافر باشد که با لب چون شکرت   امکان گنه یابد و پرهیز کند

The moment my eyes are flooded with tears
Her image, like a lustrous pearl, appears.
"Pour more wine for this dear honored guest,"
I tell my eyes, whispering in their ears.

آن لحظ کز او اشک همی رفت شتاب   در چشم آمد خیال آن در خوشاب

مهمان عزیز است بیفزای شراب   پنهان گفتم براز در گوش دو چشم

I know, when my heart steps up to speak,
It soon will be openly disgraced.
Obsessed with the memory of your beauty,
Your face appears with every breath it takes.

من می دانم که زود رسوا گردد   آن جا که بهر سخن دل ماگردد

کز هر نفسش نقش تو پیدا گردد   چندان بکند یاد جمال خوش تو

What can I do, idol? I worship your face.

Your beautiful eyes make me shy. What can I do?

Each moment I cry out in passion:

By God, I haven't a clue what to do.

من عاشق روی تو نگارم چه کنم؟   وز چشم خوش تو شرمسارم چه کنم؟

هر لحظه یکی شور برآرم چه کنم؟   والله بخدا خبر ندارم چه کنم

When I'm with you, love keeps me awake.

Without you, I can't sleep for weeping.

Good God, I'm up all night both nights,

But what a difference your presence makes.

تا با تو بوَم تخمم از یاری ها   تا بی تو بوَم تخمم از زاری ها

سبحان الله که هر دو شب بیدارم   تو فرق نگر میان بیداری ها

A thousand want to be one with you,
But for whom does that lie within reach?
Who reaches that union finds complete peace.
For the rest, the search and its pain suffice.

مر وصل تراهزار صاحب هوس است   تا خود به وصال تو که را دسترس است

آن کس که بیافت راحتی یافت تمام   و آنکس که نیافت رنج نایافت بس است

Don't shut my ears to whispered secrets.
Don't turn my eyes from my beloved's face.
Don't bar the flute and the wine from my feast.
Don't let me draw one breath without you, friend.

گوش ما را بی دم اسرار مدار   چشم ما را بی رخ دلدار مدار

بزم ما را بی نی و خمار مدار   ما را نفسی بی خودت ای یار مدار

This burning in my chest comes of following her cult.
From her I caught the fever, now I'm sick.
I'll follow doctor's orders, in all respects but this:
I won't forego the sugared wine of her lips.

این سینه پر مشعله از مکتب اوست / و امروز که بیمار شدم از تب اوست

پرهیز کنم زهر چه فرمود طبیب / جز از می و شکری که از آن از لب اوست

Show your face — we long to paint your image.
If you won't come, we're determined to go there.
Send a kiss, one by one, for each of us.
If you won't, then just send one and we can share.

یا صورت خود نمای تا نقش کنیم / یا عزم کنیم که پای در کفش کنیم

یا هر یک را جدا جدا بوسه بده / یا یک بوسه که تا هم پخش کنیم

Wrestling with the Angel

در افتادن با فرشته

When the beloved becomes jealous, demanding, fickle, imperious, unpredictable, and impossible to please, it makes for compelling drama. On the surface, many of these poems read like glimpses of a lovers' quarrel. It is here also that Rumi seems most human, reporting directly from the battlefront of an emotionally turbulent struggle of the spirit.

These are not petty fights, but tests that batter the ego and strip love down to essentials. How much rejection can the ego stand before its defenses surrender? How far are we willing to walk on a path that may have no end?

Every trial is also a gift: The jealousy of the beloved demands that the lover turn his back on all others, and the world begins to fall away.

Fear this love's force that will burn through the world.
Fear this fine cloak, so auspiciously stitched.
When he comes to you monkish, pious, contrite,
Fear the very day that he repents.

زین عشق پر از فعل جهانسوز بترس   زین تیر قبانخش کم دوز بترس
وانکه آمد چو زاهدان توبه کند   آن روز که توبه کرد، آن روز بترس

I said I'd take my heart back from you, but I can't,
Or that I'd live on without this pain, but I can't.
I said I'd banish desire for you, but I can't —
I swear to you, as I am a man, I can't.

گفتم که دل از تو بر کنم نتوانم   یا بی غم تو دمی زنم نتوانم
گفتم که ز سر برون کنم سودایت   ای خواجه اگر مردمنم نتوانم

If I was not so pitifully in love,
I wouldn't then be standing at your door.
"Go away," you say, "don't stand at my door!"
I wouldn't exist, my dear, if I didn't stand here.

گر عاشق زار روی تو نیستی   چندان بدر سرای تو نه ایستی

گفتی که مایست بر درم خیز برو   ای دوست اگر نه ایستی نیستی

Curses fall from your lips and the moon smiles.
Those curses come from rubies forged in fire.
Curse again, your words caress my heart
Like a breeze that stirs the petals of a flower.

دشنام که از لب تو مهوش باشد   چون لعل بود که اصلش آتش باشد

بر کوی که دشنام تو دلکش باشد   هر باد که بر گل گذرد خوش باشد

I spent last night with a goddess who dallies with slaves like me.
Again and again I begged, but her answer still, "We'll see."
Night passed and left our story hanging.
Was night to blame? No, our story has no ending.

من بودم و دوش آن بت بنده نواز   از من همه لابه بود و از وی همه ناز

شب رفت و حدیث ما به پایان نرسید   شب را چه گنه؟ حدیث ما بود دراز

I'm sad that as she binds me in this pain,
My love does not intend my heart to gain
Its happiness. When she sees my distress
She laughs in secret at this sweet, sweet jest.

یاری که مراد رغم خود می بندد   غمگینم از آن که خوش دلم نپسندد

چون بیند او مرا که من غمگینم   پنهان پنهان شکر شکر می خندد

I'm a slave to him who's happy without me.
The one I'm coupled to delights in solitude.
They ask me, "Do you enjoy his loyalty?"
Who knows? Even so, his cruelty delights me.

من بنده آن کسم که بی ماش خوش است   جفت آن کسم که تنهاش خوش است

گویند وفای او چه لذت دارد   زآنم خبری نیست، جفاهاش خوش است

By nature, hard as stone with a heart of steel,
Your stone and steel throw fiery sparks at me.
Moon of Khotan, flint in flame, I'd be an ass
To lay my heart down now in this dry grass.

طبع تو چو سنگ و دلت چون آهن   وز آهن و سنگ جسته آتش سوی من

سنگت چو در آتش است ای ماه ختن   خرمن باشم که دل نهم بر خرمن

I said, "I'll fly like a bird from your hand."
She said, "Fly, and you'll suffer hard my loss."
"I'm wretched," I said, "you have ruined me."
"Bear that honor," said she, "with dignity."

گفتم بجهم همچو کبوتر ز کفت   گفت ار بجهی غم سختت

گفتم که شدم خوار و زبون و تلفت   گفت از تلف تست عز و شرفت

I meant to leave for a while
So that my love might feel regret.
He was ever patient. I can't hide
That I failed, however hard I tried.

گفتم بفراق مدتی بگزارم   باشد که پشیمان شود آن دلدارم

بس نوشید ز صبر و بس کوشیدم   نتوانستم از تو چه پنهان دارم

Accept my humble service one more time.
Take pity on my weak and scattered mind.
But if I should transgress yet again,
Let my helpless cries go unheard then.

رحم آر بدین عجز و پراکندگیم   یک بار دگر قبول کن بندگیم

فریاد مرس به هیچ درماندگیم   گر بار دگر ز من خلافی بینی

My heart plays on the stage of your garden
And my candy is your bitter cruelty.
I make no complaint about this longing.
It delights me that you hear my heart moan.

شد تلخی جور هات حلوای دلم   شد گلشن روی تو تماشای دلم

ذوقی دارد که بشنوی وای دلم   ما را ز غمت شکایتی نیست و لیک

If you poked thorns into these streaming eyes,
Or shot cruel arrows at this hair-thin heart,
Or beat me like a drum and beat again,
I'd still be holding tight to your robe's hem.

ور تیر جفا بر دل چون موی زنی   گر خار بدین دیده چون جوی زنی

گر همچو دفم هزار بر روی زنی   من دست ز دامن تو کوته نکنم

I'm not a bee that flies away from smoke,
Nor a ghost that fades at burning aloes,
Nor a broken bridge, washed away by floods,
Nor avarice, lured away by profit.

یا همچو پری به بوی عودی بروم   زنبور نیم که من به دودی بروم

یا حرص که در عشوه سودی بروم   یا پل که شکسته تا بر ودی بروم

I grasp your foot, I won't let my hand go.
You've pierced my heart — what cure should I seek?
You taunt me, you say that my heart runs dry.
If so, then why does it flow from my eyes?

پای تو گرفته‌ام نذارم ز تو دست   درمان ز که جویم که دلم مهر تو خست

هی طعنه زنی که بر جگر آبت نیست   گر بر جگرم نیست چه شد بر مژه هست

Get up! Show some respect for her good name!
Speak to your lover, let her soothe your heart.
Get out of this world's trap, the other's better.
If she throws you out the door, climb through the roof!

برخیزو بکر دان نکونام درآی   در صحبت آن یار دلارام درآی

زین دام برون جه و در آن دام درآی   از در اگرت براند از بام درآی

Any thief of a kiss can have your lips free,
When it's my turn you set a high price.
Others' crimes you forgive without real cause,
But mine — you cry for the harshest of laws!

لب بر لب هر بوسه ربایی بنهی   نوبت چو بما رسد بهایی بنهی

جرم همه را عفو کنی بی سببی   وین جرم مرا دستی و پایی بنهی

However long your patience, I will shred it.
If you sleep, I'll steal the dreams from your eyes.
Stand like a mountain, I'll melt you in fire —
Be the sea and I'll drink your water dry.

گر صبر کنی پرده صبرت بدریم   ور خواب روی خواب ز چشمت ببریم

گر کوه شوی در آتشت بگدازیم   ور بحر شوی تمام آبت بخوریم

If I die in this war, this combat with you,
I won't even sigh for fear of angering you.
I'll die with a smile like a flower in your hand,
Wilting and wounded by your bloodthirsty wiles.

گر کشته شوم به رزم و پیکار تو من   آهی نکشم ز بیم آزار تو من

از زخم سر غمزه خونخوار تو من   خندان میرم چو گل ز دیدار تو من

With every breath, my love torments my wounded heart.
Hers is hard as stone, or mine remains unknown.
I've written my story with the ink my eyes bled.
My lover sees the words, but they remain unread.

هر دم دل خسته‌ام برنجاند یار   یا سنگدلست یا نمی‌داند یار

از دیده به خون نبشته‌ام قصه خویش   می‌بیند و هیچ بر نمی‌خواند یار

You, who trap me in a hundred snares —
Night comes and you say, "Go, I'll send for you."
And if I go, who will you lie with then?
Who will you call by my name, friend?

ای آن که مرا بسته صد دام کنی   گویی که به رو در شب و پیغام کنی
گر من بروم تو با که آرام کنی   هم نام من ای دوست که را نام کنی

I will break the law of pain and remedy,
Break the cycle of kind and cruel.
You saw me repent, and how sincerely —
Watch too when I break repentance's rule.

من قاعده در دو دوایی شکنم   من قاعده مهر و جفایی شکنم
دیدی که به صدق توبه‌ها می کردم   بنگر که چگونه توبه‌ها می شکنم

You've had your fill, not me. What's the remedy?
Give me a token — though what could take your place?
"Have faith," you say, "Be patient to the end."
O slave of faith! What is faith if not you?

تو سیر شدی من نشدم درمان چیست   بنما عوض خود عوض جانان چیست

گفتی که به صبر آخر ایمان داری   ای بنده ایمان به جز او ایمان چیست

I want a trouble-maker for a lover,
A spiller and drinker of blood, a heart of flame,
Who quarrels with the sky and fights with stars,
Who burns like fire on the rushing sea.

یار خواهم که فتنه انگیز بود   آتش دل و خونخواره و خونریز بود

با چرخ و ستارگان باستیز بود   در بحر رود چو آتش تیز بود

My hard friend, you ask for my heart and my gold.
The truth is, I have neither one to give.
Gold? What gold does a poor man have?
Since when does a lover have a heart left to give?

از من زر و دل خواستی ای مهر گسل   حقا که نه این دارم و نی آن حاصل

زر کو؟ زر کی؟ زر از کجا مفلس و زر   دل کو؟ دل کی؟ دل از کجا عاشق و دل؟

You fall in love, heart, and then worry for your life?
You steal and then you think of the police?
You claim to love, but it's nonsense, mere play,
If you worry what other people say.

عاشق شوی ای دل و ز جان اندیشی   دزدی کنی و ز پاسبان اندیشی

دعوی محبت کنی ای بی معنی   وانگه ز زبان این و آن اندیشی

When you set eyes upon that flower,
Your roar will fill up heaven's dome.
Thousand-year-old wine won't drive you insane
Like love that's spent one year in vain.

چشمی که نظر بدان گل ولاله کند   این کند چرخ را پر از ناله کند

می های هزار ساله هرگز نکنند   دیوانگئی که عشق یک ساله کند

If you are loyal, keeper of secrets,
Don't give the game of those lost hearts away.
It's a game, but its fire is so very real
That it kills the lover at play.

گر آن که امین و محرم این رازی   در بازی بی دلان مکن طنازی

بازیست ولیک آتش راستیش   بس عاشق را که کشت بازی بازی

Grant him a cruel and faithless lover, Lord.
Grant him a love that eats away at the heart.
Let him know for himself the sorrow love brings.
Grant him love, bliss, ecstasy – give him the whole damn thing.

یا رب تو یکی یار جفاکارش ده   یایک دلبر بدخوی جگر خوارش ده

تا بشناسد که عاشقان در چه غم اند   عشقش ده و شوقش ده و بسیارش ده

Die for Love

در عشق بمیر

THE BELOVED MAKES THE ULTIMATE DEMAND. The ego screams "Calamity! Disaster!" as it is led to the slaughterhouse.

If Islam means "submission"— submission to God's will— then its mystical tradition, the Sufi path of love, is surrender distilled to its purest essence.

This love takes no prisoners, honors no white flag. It demands we surrender all reservations, all mundane concerns, all reputation, all notions of self. It demands our very life.

In the abattoir of love, they only kill the choicest.
The small-minded, mean ones they reject.
If you love truly, don't run from the knife.
The ones they don't kill are already dead.

در مسلخ عشق جز نکو را نکشند   لاغر صفتان زشت خو را نکشند

گر عاشق صادقی ز کشتن مگریز   مردار بود هر آن که او را نکشند

My heart wanted only a kiss from you;
The price you asked for that kiss was my soul.
Heart came running, chasing after soul —
"Let's seal the deal, the price he asks is cheap!"

گفتم دلم از تو بوسه‌ای خواهانست   گفتا که بهای بوسه ما جانست

دل آمد و در پهلوی جان گشت روان   یعنی که بیا بیع و بها ارزانست

I set my heart on calamity's path.
I set it free specially to follow you.
Today the wind carried your scent to me;
So, to the wind, I gave my heart gratefully.

بر رهگذر بلا نهادم دل را   خاص از پی تو پای گشادم دل را

از باد مرا بوی تو آمد امروز   شکرانه آن به باد دادم دل را

Tangled, even briefly, in your love,
Disaster crashes down upon one's head.
Honest Mansour [3] revealed love's secret truth,
And was hung by the rope of his zeal.

با هر که دمی عشق تو آمیخته شد   گویی که بلا بر سر او ریخته شد

منصور ز سر عشق می دادنشان   حلقش به طناب غیرت آویخته شد

Not just her laugh and her face are lovely –
Her anger, her moods, her harsh words are too.
Like it or not, she demands my life.
Who cares for life? Her demand's lovely too.

تنها نه همین خنده و سیماش خوشست   خشم و سخط و طعنه و صفراش خوشست
سر خواسته من گر بدهم یا ندهم   سر را محلی نیست تقاضاش خوشست

By nightfall, what trace is left of morning?
When love's sincere, who cares for his good name?
You cry, complaining love has burned you.
Enough of crying! You're not burnt, you're raw.

ای دل اثر صبح که شام که دید   یک عاشق صادق نکونام که دید
فریاد همی زنی که من سوخته‌ام   فریاد مکن سوخته‌ای خام که دید

Harmony itself creates this discord,
Gentle comforts generate foul moods.
A royal falcon must wear an owl's mask.
Only extinction can grant a long life.

ناساز از آنیم که سازی داریم بدخوی از آنیم که نازی داریم

در صورت جغد شاهبازی داریم در عین فنا عمر درازی داریم

Inside my heart and out, all is him.
My body, blood and veins, my life is him.
There's no room here for blasphemy or faith –
There's nothing to compare, all is him.

اندر دل من درون و بیرون همه اوست اندر تن من جان و رگ و خون همه اوست

این جای چگونه کفر و ایمان گنجد بی چون باشد وجود من چون همه اوست

My heart will never seek another heart,
Or smell another flower, knowing you.
Your love has made heart's field a desert waste.
No other love than yours grows in that place.

دل بر سر تو بدل نجوید هرگز   جز وصل تو بیچ گل نبوید هرگز

صحرای دلم عشق تو شورستان کرد   تا مهر کسی دگر نروید هرگز

Like a snake encharmed, I turn and twist,
I'm tangled, like the curls of my love's hair.
What is this knot, this snare? All I know:
If I'm not tangled here, I don't exist.

چون مار ز افسون کسی می پیچم   چون طره جعد یار بر چپ پیچم

والله که ندانم این چه پیچاپیچست   این می دانم که چون نپیچم پیچم

He's lost, King, no need for check and mate,
Just be kind — he's fallen at your feet.
He's drowned in guilt, he needs no punishment;
No need, for God's sake, to retaliate.

ای شاه تو مات گشته رامات مکن   افتاده توست جز مراعات مکن

کو غرق جرمست مجازات مکن   از بهر خدا قصد مکافات مکن

If you would satisfy your beloved,
My heart, then do and say as she orders.
If she says you are cruel, don't ask why.
Don't say maybe when she asks you to die.

ای دل اگرت رضای دلبر باید   آن باید کرد و گفت کو فرماید

گر گوید خونکری مگوی از چه سبب   ور گوید جان بده مگوی کی شاید

I will hang your sun high above heaven,
And lay your harsh hands on my troubled heart.
Where you walk, where your foot touches earth,
I will lurk, just to set eyes on that dirt.

من مهر تو بر تارک افلاک نهم   دست ستم ات بر دل غمناک نهم

هر جای که بر روی زمین پای نهی   پنهان بروم دیده بر آن خاک نهم

You think that I am at my own command?
That I draw one breath, one half a breath, at will?
I'm merely a pen in my writer's hand,
A ball at the mercy of my player's skill.

می پنداری که من بفرمان خودم   یا یک نفس و نیم نفس آن خودم

مانند قلم پیش قلمران خودم   چون گوی اسیر خم چوگان خودم

You've stripped me of all signs and name, a soul
Clapping without hands like joy itself.
No place contains my soul — Where should I go?
You've made me homeless, like spirit free to flow.

بی نام و نشان چون دل و جانم کردی   بی کیف طرب دست زنانم کردی

گفتم به کجاروم که جان را جا نیست   بی جا و روان همچو روانم کردی

If my head holds one thought wise and clear, it's you.
Poor as I am, what I hold dear is you.
No matter how I see myself, I'm nothing.
Whatever I am is entirely you.

اندر سرم ار عقل و تمیز است تویی   ولنچ از من بیچاره عزیز است تویی

چندانکه بخود می نگرم هیچ نیم   بالجمله ز من هر آنچه چیز است تویی

Who could be brought down once you've raised him high?
The misery you bring, he knows as joy.
Each day the sky will raise its head
A hundred times to kiss the feet you've chained.

کی پست شود آن که بلندش تو کنی   شادان بود آنجا که نژندش تو کنی

گردون سرافراشته صد بوسه زند   هر روز بر آن پای که بندش تو کنی

You who live for this world's life alone,
Shame on you! Why do you live this way?
Don't live without love, like a lifeless corpse.
Die for love! — if you want to be alive.

ای آن که به جان این جهانی زنده   شرمت بادا، چرا چنانی زنده؟

بی عشق مباش تا نباشی مرده   در عشق بمیر تا بمانی زنده

When I die, bring my corpse to her,

And leave me there, or what remains of me.

If my love will kiss my rotting lips

Don't think it strange that I come back to life.

مرده بگذار من سپارید شما   گر من میرم مرا بیارید شما

گر زنده شوم عجب مدارید شما   گر بوسه دهد بر لب پوسیده من

Drunk on the Essence

مست گوہر وجود

STEP INTO THE TAVERN, where you are greeted by a radiantly beautiful, young SAQI. This servant, guide, and witness hands you the cup — your own heart — and pours the wine. Drink deeply of the elixir of love. This wine is the key that unlocks the doors of perception and invites you into a realm beyond rational thought.

The Sufi symbolism surrounding the tavern, SAQI, wine, and drunken ecstasy draws on Zoroastrian lore many centuries older than Islam, which forbids the use of alcohol. The memory of its origin lives in the name given to the tavern-keeper, PIR-E MOGHAN — literally, ELDER OF THE MAGI, and in the stories of Jamshid, the mythical king who invented both wine and civilization. In Jamshid's cup, the entire world was visible and the soul could see itself mirrored.

In the shadows of the tavern a pathetic figure sprawls. He is the QALANDAR, a drunkard begging for the dregs of the barrel. He has squandered livelihood, reputation, and all dignity in the service of his thirst. Defying Muslim rules of conduct, he is a humble role model (in poetry at least, if more rarely in life) for those who would avoid the trap of taking pride in their own piety.

We are drunk on the wine that needs no cup,
Aglow in the morning, ecstatic all night.
They say our path leads nowhere — so what?
We need no destination to be happy.

ماییم که از باده بی جام خوشیم   هر صبح منوریم و هر شام خوشیم

گویند سرانجام ندارید شما   ماییم که بی هیچ سرانجام خوشیم

A lover's one who must drink, day and night,
To tear off reason's veil and his own shame.
In love there are no parts — no mind, body, soul, heart.
Being one with love cannot be two.

عاشق باید که روز و شب باده خورد   تا پرده عقل و شرم خود را بدرد

در عشق تن و عقل و دل و جان نبود   هر کس که چنین یکیست دو آن نبود

Saqi, bring me wine and nothing else;
Bring the wine that wakes free men to life.
A storm is stirring in the sky, you said.
Until it pours, my love, pour wine for me.

ساقی گفتم ترا می ساده بیار   وان زنده کن مردم آزاده بیار

گفتی که در این دور فلک بادی هست   تا باد رسیدن ای صنم باده بیار

They say heaven's a sublime paradise
Where nymphs and elixirs await.
So now we grasp at love and wine
In sweet anticipation of our fate.

گویند که فردوس برین خواهد بود   آنجا می ناب و حور عین خواهد بود

پس ما می و معشوق بکف می داریم   چون عاقبت کار همین خواهد بود

This morning, with my cup of wine in hand,
I fall and rise and, drunk, again I fall.
Beside her cypress tall, I am low and small,
I'm nothing. There's nothing but her at all.

امروز من و جام صبوحی در دست / می افتم و می خیزم می گردم مست

با سرو بلند خویش من متم و پست / من نیست شوم تا نبود جزوی هست

I went to my love on a moment's thought.
She said, "Get away from my door, you're drunk."
"Open the door," I said, "I am not!"
"Go away," she said, "you are what you are."

رفتم بر یار از سر سردستی / گفتا از در برو که این دم مستی

گفتم بگشای در که من مست نیم / گفتا که برو چنانکه هستی، هستی

You are all that I've ever wanted from you.
I spread a cloth on love's table for you.
Last night I dreamt, but the memory has gone.
I woke up drunk, this is all I know.

از عشق تو خوان عشق آراسته‌ام   تا خواسته‌ام از تو تراخواسته‌ام

این می دانم که مست بر خواسته‌ام   خوابی دیدم و دوش فراموشم شد

Was such a drunk ever seen in love's tavern,
Or such shabby, broken, old vats of wine?
The courtyard's awash in wine, the sky
Overflows — was such a full cup ever seen?

خم‌ها همه در شکستهٔ توست که دید   در میکدهٔ عشق چنین مست که دید

همچون قدحی گرفته در دست که دید   صحن زمی و سقف فلک را پر می

Each day my lover comes again. She's drunk,
The cup of rioting passion in her hand.
If I take it, reason's flask will break.
If I refuse, how can I escape?

هر روزه نو برآید آن دلبر مست   با ساغر پر قنه پر شور به دست

گر بستانم قراره عقل شکست   ور نستانم ندانم از دستش رست

She clapped her hands when she saw my state:
"Drunk again, and all repentance broken!"
Repentance, like glass, is so hard to make
But once made, so easy to break.

چون دید مرا مست بهم بر زد دست   کفتا که شکست توبه باز آمد مست

چون شیشه گریست توبه ما پیوست   دشوار توان کردن و آسان بشکست

Each day I taste a sweet new draught
That makes my heart forget all flavors past.
First the must of love ferments to wine,
Then it's offered and I sip into a trance.

هر روز دلم نو شکری نوش کند کز ذوق گذشته‌ها فراموش کند

اول باده ز عاشقی نوش کند آنگاه دهد به ما و مد هوش کند

My life is lost, my world is lost — all lost.
O moon, I've lost the earth, the sky — all lost.
Don't pass the wine, just pour it in my mouth.
I've lost the very way to my own mouth.

ای جان و جهان جان و جهان گم کردم ای ماه زمین و آسمان گم کردم

می بر کف من منه به بر دهنم کز مستی تو راه دهان گم کردم

Drinking with my lover in distress,
I fell asleep without speaking my heart.
When I woke from my drunken nap, I found
My love gone, the candle out, Saqi sleeping sound.

می خوردم باده بابت آشفته   خوابم بربود حال دل ناگفته

بیدار شدم ز خواب مستی، دیدم   دلبر شده شمع مرده، ساقی خفته

I said, "You are the wine, and I the cup.
I'm lifeless; you are life itself, and sweet.
Open the door, trust me." "Hush!" said she,
"Let a madman loose in the house? What for?"

گفتم که تویی می و من ام پیمانه   من مرده ام و تو جانی و جانانه

اکنون بگشا در وفا گفت خموش   دیوانه کسی رها کند در خانه؟

Luminous full moon, the bow of your brow
Shoots an arrow, and fills heart's flask with blood.
"This flask, this blood — what could compare?" I ask.
"There" — she offers the cup of wine — "take it."

زان ابروی چون کانت ای بدر منیر   دل شیشه پر خون شود از ضربت تیر

گویم ز دل و شیشه و خون چیست نظیر   بردارد جام باده و گوید گیر

I swear by the heart that is humbled by her;
I swear by the soul that's besotted with her;
I swear by the moment they saw me,
A jug in one hand, her hand in the other.

سوگند بدان دل که شده است او پستش   سوگند بدان جان که شده است او مستش

سوگند بدان دم که مرا می دیدند   پیمانه بدستی و بدستی دستش

Until you made me sing, I was a monk.
You made me a drunkard, a rabble-rouser.
I used to sit in prayer, so dignified.
Now I'm a toy that children toss aside.

سر حلقهٔ بزم و باده جویم کردی   زاهد بودم ترانه گویم کردی

بازیچهٔ کودکان کویم کردی   سجاده نشین با وقارم کردی

We have no fear of arrows or daggers,
Or shackles, or the blade against the neck.
Hotheaded, we drink the devil's drink.
Even less, we fear what people think.

وز بستن پای و رفتن سر ترسیم   جائی که ز زخم تیر و خنجر ترسیم

از گفت و گوی خلق کمتر ترسیم   ما گرم روان و دوزخ آشنائیم

My faith in God is this: her eyes, their cheer,
Their drunken joy, and her wild, heathen hair.
They say this cannot be true religion.
If so, with true religion I break faith.

مامذهب چشم شوخ مستش داریم   کیش سر زلف بت پرستش داریم

گویند جز این هر دو بود دین درست   از دین درست ما شکستش داریم

"So what?" says the charming flirt to accusing eyes,
And the love-struck fool to his bad name: "So what?"
As we become sure-footed on love's path
So what if those lame donkeys stumble behind?

از دیده گری، دلبر عنا راچه؟   وز بد نامی، عاشق شیدا راچه؟

ما در ره عشق چست و چالاک شویم   ور زانکه خری لنگ شود، ما راچه؟

Penniless and ragged, we are happy,
Content in pain, and in fear still happy,
With surrender's wine, happy for all time —
Don't assume we're like you, only halfway happy.

ماییم که بی قماش و بی سیم خوشیم   در رنج مرفهیم و دردیم خوشیم

تا دور ابد از می تسلیم خوشیم   تا ظن نبری که ما چو تو نیم خوشیم

Alone
in the Desert

تنها در صحرای بی کسی

RUMI AND SHAMS SPENT A YEAR and more in close company. And then Shams disappeared, driven away by the jealous machinations of Rumi's followers.

More essentially, Shams's decision to leave Rumi arose from the knowledge that his own absence was necessary for his beloved pupil to grow in wisdom. "I'm not in the position to order you to go on a journey," Shams wrote, "so it is I who will be obliged to go away for the sake of your development, for separation makes a person wise."[4]

Beyond fortitude and self-reliance there should be compassion too in this wisdom, for separation from the divine is the common human condition. A baby cries at birth because its soul realizes its separation from God. Having tasted union, its loss is the more painful.

He's gone – there has never been so good a friend;
Gone before my heart was full or ready for an end.
He's gone, and with him, the cure for this pain.
The rose is gone and still the thorn remains.

رفت آن که نبود کس به خوبی یارش   بی آن که دل ام سیر شد از دیدارش

او رفت و نماند در دلم تیمارش   آری برود گل و بماند خارش

You pitched your tent of moonlight on the darkness,
Then threw water on wisdom when it dreamt.
You lulled us, promised sleep with one eye cocked,
Then, with goodbye's blade, you cut sleep's throat.

بر ظلمت شب خیمه مهتاب زدی   میخفت خرد بر رخ او آب زدی

دادی همه را به وعده خواب خرگوشی   وز تیغ فراق کردن خواب زدی

Last night I said your leaving me was misery;
This world that trades in separation troubles me.
I saw myself coupled with your fantasy,
So I took my dream of you to sleep with me.

من دوش فراق را جفا می گفتم   با دهر فراق پیشه می آشفتم
خود را دیدم که با خیالت جفتم   با جفت خیال تو بر فتم خفتم

My friend, in friendship I am bound to you:
Wherever you set foot, I am the ground.
Since when do the laws of love allow
That I may see your world, but not see you?

ای دوست بدوستی قرینیم ترا   هر جا که قدم نهی زمینیم ترا
در مذهب عاشقی روا کی باشد   عالم تو ببینیم و نه بینیم ترا

"The snare of those curls won't catch you
When you're drunk on the wine of her eyes,"
My enemies taunt me, night and day.
"You tripped and fell, she never took your hand."

گر حلقهٔ آن زلف چو پشتت نگرفت   تا باده از آن دو چشم مستت نگرفت

می طعنه زنند دشمنانم شب و روز   کز پای در آمدی و دستت نگرفت

The suffering one to whom you offered justice,
The sad one whom you served happiness,
Has forgotten that first wine's taste.
If you pour no more, then why remind him?

آن ظلم رسیده‌ای که دادش دادی   وان غم زده‌ای که جام شادش دادی

آن بادهٔ اولین فراموشش شد   گر باز نمی دهی چه یادش دادی؟

Remembering your lips, I kiss the ruby on my ring;

One I cannot reach, I kiss the one I can.

My hand can't touch your distant sky,

And so I bow full low and kiss the ground.

بر یاد لب ات لعل نگین می بوسم		آنم چو به دست نیست این می بوسم

دستم چو بر آسمان تو می نرسد		می آرم سجده و زمین می بوسم

Remembering your scent, when I see a flower

I smell it and tears begin to pour.

When I see a cypress in the meadow,

I kiss its feet in memory of you.

بر بوی تو هر کجا گلی دیدم		بوئیدم، سرشک باریدم

در هر چمنی که دیده ام سروی را		بر یاد قد تو پایش بوسیدم

Waiting for news of her, I sleep.
But who can sleep when news of her arrives?
All night long, love speaks in both my ears:
"Shame on him who sleeps alone without her."

آن سر که بود بی خبر از وی خسبد   آن کس که خبر یافت از او کی خسبد

می گوید عشق در دو گوشم همه شب   ای وای بر آن کسی که بی وی خسبد

I journeyed through the desert of your love,
Searching for some hint that you might join me.
I saw in every home I passed along the way
Scattered corpses of those who went before me.

در بادیه عشق تو کردم سفری   تا بو که بیابم ز وصالت خبری

در هر منزل که می نهادم قدمی   افکنده تنی دیدم و افتاده سری

The day I'll join my lover is nowhere in sight,
So little by little I must give up this love.
"Impossible!" my heart cries out, "Impossible!"
She shakes her head and tries to hide a smile.

چون روز وصال یار مانیست پدید   اندک اندک ز عشق باید ببرید

می گفت دلم که این محالست محال   سر پیش فکنده، زیر لب می خندید

Now that I can't touch the dust at your door,
The company I keep are cries and groans.
I'm a candle dripping dignified tears,
I'm a harp making music from moans.

از خاک در تو چون جدا می باشم   با گریه و ناله آشنا می باشم

چون شمع ز گریه آب رو می دارم   چون چنگ ز ناله با نوا می باشم

Reciting you, friend, I lose sight of you.
Your dear face is veiled by the light of you.
I remember your lips, but the memory —
The memory, friend, veils your lips from me.

ای ذکر تو مانع تماشای تو دوست   برق رخ تو نقاب سیمای تو دوست

بایاد لبت از لب تو محرومم   ای یاد لبت حجاب لب های تو دوست

Everyone has someone, a friend to love,
Work to be done and the skill to do it.
I have only love's mirage, lodged in my heart
Like a holy man hiding in a cave.

هر کس کسی دارد و هر کس یاری   هر کس هنری دارد و هر کس کاری

ماییم و خیال یار و این گوشهٔ دل   چون احمد و بوبکر بکوشهٔ غاری

When there's no sign of hope in the desert,
So much hope still lives inside despair.
Heart, don't kill that hope. Even willows bear
Sweet fruit in the garden of the soul.

گر هیچ نشانه نیست اندر وادی   بیار امیدهاست در نومیدی

ای دل مبر امید که در روضه جان   خرما دهی ار نیز درخت بیدی

Reunion

بازآئی

INCONSOLABLE AT THE LOSS OF SHAMS, Rumi withdrew into his grief. Their teacher's misery caused at least some of his fractious disciples to repent, and efforts were made to locate Shams. False sightings raised and then dashed Rumi's hopes.

When a letter from Shams reached him, it unleashed a torrent of poetry in reply. Finally, a search party led by Rumi's younger son, Sultan Valad, discovered Shams in Damascus, and convinced him to return. On his arrival in Konya, Rumi welcomed his friend with a joyful celebration of their reunion.

There's joy in my heart — I've joined my beloved tonight;
Finally free from the pain of our parting tonight.
As we spin in dance, I pray in my heart: O Lord,
May the keys to morning be lost forever tonight.

هستم بوصال دوست دلشاد امشب   وز غصه هجر گشته آزاد امشب
با یار بجرخم و دل می گوید   یارب که کلید صبح گم باد امشب

He's come! He who never left us has come!
The water never dried up from this stream.
He's the pod of musk and I'm its perfume.
How could the scent be cut off from its source?

آمد آمد آن که نرفت او هرگز   بیرون ندید آن آب از این جو هرگز
او نافه مشک و ما همه بوی ویم   از نافه شنیده ای جدا بو هرگز

Eternity's sea is a drop of you,

Heaven's moon, a glimmer of your brilliance.

I long for this light to last the long night –

Your face shines in the night sky of your hair.

ای آب حیات قطره‌ای ز آب رخ ات   وی ماه فلک یک اثر از تاب رخ ات

گفتم که شب دراز خواهم مهتاب   آن شب، شب زلف توست و مهتاب رخ ات

That king who drove me mad, and with whom

My heart, for love of him, has shared a home,

Sent a moth that signified, "I'm yours,"

And fanned a hundred candles into flame.

آن شاه که هست عقل دیوانه او   وز عشق دلم شده است همخانه او

پروانه فرستاد که من آن توام   صد شمع بسوز رشد ز پروانه او

My face was pale, my heart was overflowing
And traveled the same path that Majnoon trod.[5]
That was how things stood until this moment –
What's happened now turns all that to nothing.

اول که رخم زرد و دلم پر خون بود   هم خرقه و همراه دلم مجنون بود

آن صورت و آن قاعده تا اکنون بود   کاری آمد که آن همه مادون بود

O heart, now that you have joined your friend,
Why do you still moan? Extinguish yourself
Before this exalted longing. The sun
Has shown its face – put out your candle now.

ای دل چو وصال یار دیدی حالی   در پای غمش بمیر تا کی نالی

شرطست چو آفتاب رخ بنماید   گر شمع نمیرد بکشندش حالی

Treasure, come home quickly to your ruins.
Curls, don't fly in disarray from your own comb.
Bird, don't turn away, this seed is yours.
House of God, come home to your own home.

ای گنج بیا زود بویرانهٔ خویش   وی زلف پریشان مشو از شانهٔ خویش

وی مرغ متاب روی از دانهٔ خویش   ای خانهٔ خدا درآئی در خانهٔ خویش

I told my heart, "If there's a chance to speak,
Tell my love, among your words, my longing."
Heart answered, "When my friend and I unite,
My gaze does not concern itself with speech."

بادل گفتم اگر بود جای سخن   بادوست غمم بگو در اثنای سخن

دل گفت نگاه وصل بایار مرا   نبود ز نظاره هیچ پروای سخن

I'm not me, you're not you, and you're not me,
And yet I'm me, you're you, and you are me.
Beauty of Khotan, I am this because of you:[6]
Confused if I am you or you are me.

نی من منم ونی تو توئی نی تو منی   هم من منم وهم تو توئی هم تو منی

من با تو چنانم ای نگار ختنی   کاندر غلطم که من توام یا تو منی

Gentle hearts, who scatter seeds of loyalty
And rain pure goodness down on this black earth,
You've heard, no matter where, the state I'm in —
Don't separate me from my love again.

ای نرم دلانی که وفامی کارید   بر خاک سیه در صفامی بارید

در هر جائی خبر ز حالم دارید   در دست چنین هجر مرا مگذارید

I've never seen a greener tree than you.
I've never seen a brighter moon than you.
I've never seen the sun rise more eagerly
Or sweetness more delicious than you.

سرسبزتر از تو من ندیدم شجری   پرنورتر از تو من ندیدم قمری
شبخیزتر از تو من ندیدم سحری   پر ذوق تر از تو من ندیدم شکری

In the Garden

در باغ

THE PERSIAN GARDEN is modeled on the plan of paradise, with which it shares its name. Protected by walls from the desert wilderness, it is an interior as much as an exterior space, and a convivial one: the setting for conversation, wine, and song beside flowing streams. Its riot of color is the world's dream, all life contained, the screen on which the sun — in Arabic, SHAMS — projects its light.

Rumi's representation of nature, as in all Persian poetry, is as stylized as a carpet motif that has been rewoven for generations. Its art lies not in the fresh and particular observation, but in the power of the archetype. Spring would not stir the heart but for the certainty of its hope's fulfillment year after year, no matter how long and dark the winter.

The nightingale comes to the garden, no more the crow.
Light of my eyes, to the garden with you I'll go.
Like lilies, like roses, we'll open in blossom.
A stream running from garden to garden, we'll flow.

بلبل آمد به باغ و رستیم ز زاغ   آییم به باغ با توای چشم و چراغ

چون سوسن و گل ز خویش بیرون آییم   چون آب روان رویم از باغ به باغ

Greeting dawn in the garden, picking flowers,
I was startled when the gardener came in view.
"What's a flower worth?" — sweet words
He said — "I gave the whole garden to you."

در باغ شدم صبوح و گل می چیدم   از دیدن باغبان همی ترسیدم

شیرین سخنی ز باغبان بشنیدم   گل را چه محل، باغ به تو بخشیدم

That daffodil wept tears like wine for me,

Till I was amazed to see them flow.

The paint would run dark rivers down her cheeks

If those dark eyes were merely painted so.

بر من بگریست نرگس خمارش   تا خیره شدم ز گریه بسیارش

گر نرگس او بسرمه آلوده بدی   آلوده شدی ز سرمه‌ها رخسارش

A thousand brilliant beauties filled the garden.

There were musk-scented roses and violets

And water rippling rings in the stream.

All this was just pretense — everything was him.

در باغ هزار شاهد مه رو بود   گلها و بنفشه‌های مشکین بو بود

وان آب ذره ذره که اندر جو بود   این جمله بهانه بود و او خود او بود

Heart, if you sit in the thorns and choose
Not to pick flowers, what can I do?
His splendor lights up the world.
If you can't see it, what can I do?

ای دل چو بهر خسی نشینی چه کنم   وز باغ مدام گل نچینی چه کنم

عالم همه از جمال او روشن شد   تو دیده نداری که ببینی چه کنم

My love, will I tire of you? Never.
Or ever love another? Never.
In the garden we share, I see roses.
Do the thorns bewilder me? Never.

جانا ز تو بیزار شوم نی نی نی   با جز تو دگر یار شوم نی نی نی

در باغ وصالت چو همه گل بینم   سرگشته بهر خار شوم نی نی نی

This blooming branch will bend with fruit one day.
This falcon too will grasp its prey one day.
His image approaches you, then flies away,
Till it rests firm in mind at last one day.

این شاخ شکوفه بار گیرد روزی   وین باز طلب شکار گیرد روزی

می‌آید می‌رود خیالش بر تو   تا چند رود قرار گیرد روزی

What you've planted will ripen if you water me.
If you mow me down, it's because you've raised me.
I was dusty earth under thorn and scrub.
Because of you, Moon, I touch the heavens.

گر آب دهی نهال خود کاشته‌ای   ور پست کنی مرا تو برداشته‌ای

خاکی بودم بزیر پاهای خسان   همچون فلکم مه‌ا تو افراشته‌ای

My tender moon, soul's bountiful harvest,
You bow your head to enter my window.
Bright light of my eyes, my soul's rose garden,
When will you wrap me in your embrace?

ای ماه لطیف جانفزا خرمن من   وی ماه فرو کرده سر از روزن من

ای گلشن جان و دیده روشن من   کی ینت آویخته بر گردن من؟

That garden, whose springtime made me blossom,
Bloomed itself, displaying all I'd said.
When he pressed luck's blessed cup on me,
My head reeled and I laid down to rest.

باغی که من از بهار او بشکفتم   بشکفت و نمود هر چه من می گفتم

با ساغر اقبال چو کرد او جفتم   سرمست شدم سر بنهادم خفتم

Why be content to smile with lips pressed tight?
You should laugh like a flower without a care.
Love that leaps from the soul is not the same
As love you tie to yourself with a string.

با خنده بربسته چرا خرسندی چون گل باید که بی تکلف خندی

فرصت میان عشق کز جان خیزد یا آنچه بریسمانش بر خود بندی

My love, there's a path from your heart to mine,
And my heart knows how to find it,
For my heart now is a pool, sweet and clear,
That serves the moon as her mirror.

ای جان ز دل تو بر دل من راهست وز جستن آن در دل من آگاه است

زیرا دل من چو آب صافی خوش است آب صافی آینه دار ماه است

With a beautiful voice, a nightingale
Sang by a stream, "With rubies, emeralds,
Gold and perfume, you can craft a flower,
But it won't have a flower's true bloom."

دی بلبلکی لطیفکی خوشگویی   می گفت ترانه ای کنار جویی

کز لعل و زمرد و زر و زیره توان   برساخت گلی ولی ندارد بویی

Sadness and worry fade and do not last
Where wine and song and good kebab are found.
Drink the pleasure, friends, that never ends —
Kiss the water's lips, like flowers, like grass.

اندیشه و غم را نبود هستی و تاب   آنجا که شراب است و ربابست و کباب

عیش ابدی نوش کنید ای اصحاب   چون سبزه و گل نهید لب بر لب آب

You, who make all my hardship easy
And the garden, trees, flowers, drunk with your gifts —
The roses delirious, the thorns disorderly —
Pour us a cup and we will join them too.

ای آن که ز تو مشکلم آسان گردد   سرو و گل و باغ مست احسان گردد

گل سرمست و خار بدمست و خمار   جامی در ده که جمله یکسان گردد

Get up! Let's fill the night with moonlight.
Wake the flowers! Make them burn the midnight oil.
For three months we steered our ship through the ice —
Brothers, now it's time for the open sea.

خیزید که تا بر شب مهتاب زنیم   بر باغ گل و نرگس بی خواب زنیم

کشتی دو سه ماه بر سر یخ راندیم   وقت است برادران که بر آب زنیم

The Wisdom of Insanity

عقل در جنون

IF THE RATIONAL MIND casts a veil over the heart's truth, then madness is the heart unveiled in revelation of a deeper truth.

The madman has not only turned away from all human company, aside from his beloved, but is a stranger even to himself. He needs no nourishment beyond love, and sleep, too, is alien to him — this insanity is a state of awakening. Like the drunken QALANDAR, the madman holds a fearless disregard for social convention.

Wherever Arabic, Persian, or Turkish is spoken, the quintessential love story is the legend of Leyla and Majnoon, better known even than our Romeo and Juliet. When Majnoon — whose name means "insane" — was separated from his beloved Leyla, he spent the remainder of his life wandering alone in the desert. He spoke in poetry and wild animals were gentle in his presence.

When your love drives me crazy, that day
I dare things, madly, that demons would not.
Your eyelash alone does to my heart
What the pen of the scribe of fate cannot.

روزی که مرا عشق تو دیوانه کند   دیوانگیی کنم که دیوان نکند

حکم مژه تو آن کند بادل من   کز نوک قلم خواجه دیوان نکند

Love's intoxication, my disintegration —
My heart's beyond the need for food or sleep.
My body floats at sea, my feet and head
Are nowhere to be found, my soul has fled.

مستم ز می عشق خراب افتاده   بر خواسته دل از خور و خواب افتاده

در دریایی که پا و سر پیدا نیست   جان رفته و تن بر سر آب افتاده

Today's the day for courage, wounded heart —
In our love, what room is there for distance?
Whatever logic holds, put that aside —
Now's the time for madness, right this instant!

هان ای دل خسته روز مردانگیست در عشق تو‌ام چه جای بیگانگیست

هر چیزی که در تصرف عقل آید بگذار کنون که وقت دیوانگیست

I am hungry, but elated as if I were sated.
I'm only a fox, but infamous as a lion.
A part of me flinches at phantoms,
But don't look there — my soul is brave at heart.

من گرسنه‌ام نشاط سیری دارم روباهم و نام و ننگ شیری دارم

نفسی است مرا که از خیالی برمد آن را مگر، جای دلیری دارم

The mind's wealth is the secret of madness –
A wise man loves until he's insane.
He's familiar with the heart's painful path,
Yet a thousand ways a stranger to himself.

سرمایهٔ عقل سرّ دیوانگیست   دیوانهٔ عشق مرد فرزانگیست

آن کس که شد آشنای دل از ره درد   با خویشتنش هزار بیگانگیست

To the seeker, wisdom and madness are one.
In love's way, self and other are the same.
Having drunk the wine of oneness with my love,
I find the road to Mecca and Bodhgaya are the same.[7]

در راه طلب عاقل و دیوانه یکیست   در شیوهٔ عشق خویش و بیگانه یکیست

آن را که شراب وصل جانان دادند   در مذهب او کعبه و بتخانه یکیست

Don't even think, just let yourself dream.
Thoughts are veils that hide the moon's bright face.
The heart is a moon, where thinking has no place.
Toss these thoughts away into the stream.

اندیشه مکن بکن تو خود را در خواب   کاندیشه ز روی مه حجابست حجاب

دل چون ماهست در دل اندیشه مدار   انداز تو اندیشه گری را در آب

Reason came forward to lecture the lovers,
Like a bandit in ambush he lay.
But he saw that their heads had no room for reason,
So bowed at their feet and went away.

عقل آمد و پند عاشقان پیش گرفت   در ره بنشست و رهزنی کیش گرفت

چون در سرشان جایگه پندیدند   پای همه بوسید و ره خویش گرفت

Go away, logic, you have no place here,
No room for your fine split hairs.
The day has come, the sun's bright flame
Shames any lamp you have lit.

ای عقل برو که عاقلی اینجا نیست گر موی شوی موی ترا گنجانیست

روز آمد و روز هر چراغی که فروخت در شعله آفتاب جز رسوانیست

I told her, "Your love is driving me mad.
Will your curls ever chain me in my sleep?"
"Hush!" she said, "Enough of this fantasy,
Don't talk nonsense – how could a madman sleep?"

گفتم که ز عشقت شده ام دیوانه زنجیر ترا بخواب بینم یانه

گفتا که خمش چند از این افسانه دیوانه و خواب خه ای فرزانه

"You are mad," you said, "a wandering fool."
It's you who are mad, wanting me to be sane.
"You are shameless," you said, "and cold as steel."
Polish this steel — you'll see your face.

گفتی که تو دیوانه و مجنون خویی   دیوانه تویی که عقل از من جویی

گفتی که چه میشرم و چه آهن رویی   آیینه کند همیشه آهن رویی

Anyone with even a speck of a heart
Would live a hard life without your love.
The locks of your hair chain a logical man
With knot upon knot, till he goes insane.

در سینه هر که ذره ای دل باشد   بی عشق تو زندگیش مشکل باشد

باز لف چو زنجیر گره بر گره ات   دیوانه کسی بود که عاقل باشد

I'm insane, and therefore sleep is a sin.
How could a lunatic find the path to sleep?
God sleeps not and is the purer for it,
So God's mad bedmate keeps himself awake.

دیوانه چه داند که ره خواب کجاست   دیوانه شدم خواب ز دیوانه خطاست

مجنون خدا بدان هم از خواب جداست   زیرا که خدا نخفت و پاکست ز خواب

I went to my doctor and said, "Zein al-Din,
Please take my pulse and examine my urine."
"You're inflamed," said he, "with insanity."
"So be it," I said, "May it last. Let it be."

این نبض مرا بگیر و قارو ره ببین   رفتم بطبیب و گفتم ای زین الدین

گفتم حله تا باد چنین باد چنین   گفتا که بادست با جنون گشته قرین

Today I'm going to ramble drunk in town,
And drink from the bowl of a human skull.
I'll search for a wise and sensible man,
And turn him into a crazy fool.

امروز یکی گردش مستانه کنم   وز کاسه سر ساغر و پیمانه کنم

امروز در این شهر همی گردم مست   می جویم عاقلی که دیوانه کنم

Passing Shadows

سایه‌های گذرا

Even Rumi has moments of self-doubt and hesitation, fatigue and annoyance. The jealous scheming of disciples who were eager to be rid of Shams was a constant thorn in his side.

Many of the quatrains in the Divan-e Shams offer glimpses of simple human vulnerability. Others hint at personal history and circumstances that we may never know.

"Devour the garden's bounty," says heart,
"Feed in the morning and feast again tonight."
"Not so bold!" says mind, biting its lip.
"The blessings are real, but trouble still may strike."

دل می گوید که نقد این باغ دریم . امروز چریدیم و بشب هم بچریم

لب می گزدش عقل که گستاخ مرو . گرچه در رحمت است زحمت بریم

Flowing tears, speak to my garden, to him
Who makes my heart grow, my pageant of spring,
Say, "If some night, you remember those nights,
Please don't remember how rude I have been."

ای اشک روان بگو دل افزای مرا . آن باغ و بهار و آن تماشای مرا

چون یاد کنی شبی تو شب های مرا . اندیشه مکن بی ادبی های مرا

The jealous birds complained to Solomon,
Demanding he punish the nightingale.
"Calm down," she said, "I only sing in spring.
Nine months of the year I make no sound."

مرغان رقصند بر سلیمان بخروش   کاین بلبل را چرا نمی مالی گوش
بلبل گفتا نخورم مادر بجوش   سه ماه سخن گویم و نه ماه خموش

If I wait patiently, I miss you terribly.
If I speak of love openly, jealousy claws.
So I hold myself back — then stone hits glass:
"Does your love for me cause you shame?" you ask.

گر صبر کنم دل از غمت تنگ آید   ور فاش کنم حسود در چنگ آید
پرهیز کنم که شیشه بر سنگ آید   گویی که ز عشق ما ترا ننگ آید

Your soul needs to be broken and crushed,
You ought to be mocked and shamed.
If you're human, make peace with the human race.
If you claim to be an angel, go to heaven.

بیار تراخته روان باید شد   و انگشت نمای این و آن باید شد

گر آدمینی بساز با آدمیان   ور خود ملکی بر آسمان باید شد

He came fuming and frowning – "Enough!"
As if he thought I feared authority.
The heart's bird that cannot be caged
Fears no one, so don't even try.

آمد آمد ترش ترش یعنی بس   می پندارد که من بترسم ز عسس

آن مرغ دلی که نیست در بند قفس   او را تو مترسان که بترسد از کس

I entered your garden, but not to gather
Anything — a dervish, empty-handed.
Do you want me to go? Open the door.
If you won't, don't assume that I'm a thief.

در باغ تو در نیامدم گرد آور   درویش و تهی روم من راهگذر

خواهی که برون روم مرا بگشای در   ور نگشائی گمان بد نیز مبر

My nature won't let me bond with a friend,
Nor my judgment restrain me from love.
My hands can't grasp this misfortune,
Nor can my feet run away.

طبعی نه که با دوست در آمیزم من   عقلی نه که از عشق بپرهیزم من

دستی نه که با قضا در آویزم من   پایی نه که از میانه بگریزم من

Not for a moment, my heart, did you bow

To His glory, or ever rue your sin.

Mystic, ascetic, scholar of law —

These you were, but not a true Muslim.

ای دل تو دمی مطیع سبحان نشدی   وز کار بدت هیچ پشیمان نشدی

صوفی و فقیه و زاهد و دانشمند   این جمله شدی ولی مسلمان نشدی

I'm the source of such rot, such stupidity,

That because of me no one lives happily.

I demand justice — who gets it from me?

I shout at them all, they all shout at me.

از بس که فساد و ابلهی زاد از من   در عمر کسی نگشت دلشاد از من

من طالب داد و جمله بیداد از من   فریاد من از جمله و فریاد از من

No one solves this problem for me, shows me
Which way leads to water, which to mud.
Fear fills my heart with blood, the road splits here
And I must choose – Which way will take me home?

حل می نکنند هیچ کسی مشکل من کس می ندهد نشان آب و گل من

از بیم سر دو راه خون شد دل من تا خود بکدام سو بود منزل من

The ravishing moon last night shone on me –
"Not tonight," I told her, "go away."
She left saying, "Well done, gloomy one!
Treasure knocks and you don't open the door."

آمد بر من دوش مه یغمایی گفتم که برو که امشب این جانایی

می رفت و همی گفت زهی سودایی دولت به در آمده است و در نگشایی

My beloved could tear my skin away —
I won't cry out or say he's caused this pain.
I've enemies aplenty, only him for friend —
To foe concerning friend I won't complain.

دلدار اگر مرا بدرند از پوست   افغان مکنم نگویم این درد از اوست

ما را همه دشمنند و تنها او دوست   از دوست به دشمنان بنالم نه نکوست

On a wild steed with a broken bridle,
I gallop through a valley of terror
Like a bird flying flushed from a trap —
Where does this horse race to? What home, where?

من همچو کسی نشسته بر اسب رخام   در وادی هولناک بگسسته لگام

تازد چون مرغ تا که بجهد از دام   تا منزل این اسب کدام است کدام

Burning in the Flame

سوختن در شعله‌ها

A YEAR AFTER HIS RETURN, Shams disappeared again. This time Rumi himself traveled twice to Damascus to search for him, but in vain. Shams had vanished from the face of the earth. There were rumors of murder, even at the hand of Rumi's own son. As the story was repeated through history, these rumors acquired the force of fact, though they are absent from the earliest accounts.

Sorrow reaches a new fever pitch in these poems, treading the path of sadness and pain again and again in search of the beloved. Still, they are not complaints. There is no hope of solace, only of redemption. Pain is love's price, just as the moth flying into the flame pays with singed wings. It is the alchemist's fire that burns away impurity, transmuting lead into gold.

The many sighs your loss has dragged from me
Can only gratify my enemy.
Soul of my world, the pain of your going
Breaks my heart without yours even knowing.

از بس که برآورد غمت آه از من   ترسم که شود بکام بدخواه از من

دردا که ز هجران تو ای جان جهان   خون شد دلم و دلت نه آگاه از من

If you want victory, eternity,
Then burn in the fire of love, don't sleep.
You slept a hundred nights and what did you gain?
For God's sake, don't sleep tonight till dawn.

گر می خواهی بقا و پیروز محب   از آتش عشق دوست میسوز محب

صد شب خفتی و حاصل آن دیدی   از بهر خدا امشب تا روز محب

Sadness to me is the happiest time,
When cities rise from the ruins of my mind.
When I'm silent and still as the earth,
My thunder's roar fills the universe.

آنم که چو غمخوار شوم من شادم   وان دم که خراب گشته‌ام آبادم
آن لحظه که ساکن و خموشم چو زمین   چون رعد به چرخ می‌رسد فریادم

Heart, in this hard time let me share secrets.
Soul, bow your head down in agreement.
Patience, you can't stand this pain — run away.
Reason, you're only a child — go play.

ای دل تو در این واقعه دم سازی کن   وی جان به موافقت سراندازی کن
ای صبر تو پای غم نداری بگریز   ای عقل تو کودکی برو بازی کن

If my heart's not on fire, then why all this smoke?
If there's no incense burning, what do I smell?
Why this existence? — I love, I am nothing.
Why is the moth content in the flame?

گر آتش دل نیست پس این دود چراست؟   ور عود نسوخت بوی این عود چراست؟
این بودن من عاشق و نابود چراست؟   پروانه ز سوز شمع خوشنود چراست؟

Tonight, when love's longing is lasting and sustained,
The cup of ruby wine is my pillar, my strength.
Renunciation's pain and contemplation are allowed.
Sleep — even drowsiness — is forbidden.

امشب که غم عشق مدامست مدام   جام می لعل با قوامست قوام
خون غم و اندیشه حلال است حلال   خواب و هوس خواب حرامست حرام

When first that beauty stole my love from me,
My crying kept the neighbors up all night.
I cry less now that my love has grown —
The fire that gets more air makes less smoke.

زاول که مرا عشق نگارم ربود ⁣   همسایه من ز ناله من نغنود

اکنون کم شد ناله عشقم بفزود ⁣   آتش چو هوا گرفت کم گردد دود

My heart, if you can't take the sorrow, go.
The streets are full of vagrant lovers, go.
My soul, come now, if you are not afraid,
But if you fear, your work is not here, go.

ای دل اگرت طاقت غم نیست برو ⁣   آواره عشق چون توکم نیست برو

ای جان تو بیا اگر نخواهی ترسید ⁣   ور می ترسی کار تو هم نیست برو

They ask me, "Why are you in so much pain?
Why do you wail? Why is your face so pale?"
I say, "Don't tell me what I do is wrong.
Look at that moon's face — these problems fade."

گویند مرا که این همه درد چراست وین نعره و آواز و رخ زرد چراست

گویم که چنین مکو که این کار خطاست رو روی مهش بین و مشکل برخاست

If you can resist, don't wear love's robe —
If you wear it, don't moan about disaster.
The cloth will burn — bear that pain in silence.
In the end, what once stung becomes nectar.

تا توانی تو جامه عشق مپوش چون پوشیدی ز هر بلایی مخروش

در جامه هی سوز و هی باش خموش کاخر ز پس نیش بود روزی نوش

Tonight is a night of weakness, misery.
Tonight I grapple with heart's mystery.
Its secrets, my friend, are all thoughts of you.
O night, pass quickly — I have work to do.

امشب شب من بسی ضعیف و زار است امشب شب پرداختن اسرار است

اسرار دلم جمله خیال یار است ای شب بگذر زود که مرا کار است

Even if I were in hell, if I held
Your hair in my hands, I would not care
For heaven. Even if I were there,
My heart would find its wide fields too small.

در دوزخ ار ز زلف تو در چنگ آید از حال بهشتیان مرا ننگ آید

گویی که به صحرای بهشتم ببرند صحرای بهشت بر دلم تنگ آید

If one day you pass my humble mound,
Stop and say, "My love, whom sorrow killed —"
From the blood-soaked field I'll cry out loud,
"My Joseph, who was lost and now is found."[8]

روزی که گذر کنی بحر پشته من   بنشین و بکو که ای بغم کشته من

تا بانگ زنم ز خاک آغشته به خون   کای یوسف روزگار و گمگشته من

May grief and sorrow come to unfaithful hearts.
May their numbers decline in the world.
The only friend who visits me is sadness —
And for that, loyal sadness, endless thanks.

اندر دل بی وفا غم و ماتم باد   آنرا که وفانیست ز عالم کم باد

دیدی که مرا هیچ کسی یاد نکرد   جز غم که هزار آفرین بر غم باد

Sorrow refines and cleanses your soul,
It wears away your body till it's pure.
This fire of love in which you burn
Will be your garden paradise one day.

ای جان منزه ز غم پالودن
وی جسم مقدس ز غم فرسودن

این آتش عشقی که در آن میسوزی
خود جنت و فردوس تو خواهد بودن

The Open Embrace

آغوش باز

WHEN THE FLAMES have finished burning, what remains is cooked, the raw transformed. The Sufi path of love reaches its destination in a mature state that transcends individual human relationships and embraces all existence.

In coming to peace with Shams's disappearance and eventually with his death, Rumi becomes aware that his own existence encompasses what he had sought from Shams. He carries the sun within himself.

The view illuminated by this sun stretches beyond the boundaries of a personal lifetime. Releasing the bonds not only of the body, it moves also beyond heart — the domain of emotions, the self that suffers and learns — and into the realm of pure soul. Here separation has not ended. It never existed at all.

If I hold you in my heart, you'll wither,
Become a thorn if I hold you in my eyes.
I'll make room for you in my soul instead –
You'll be my love in lives beyond this life.

در دل نگذارمت که انکار شوی   در دیده ندارمت که بس خار شوی

در جان کنمت جای نه در دیده و دل   تا در نفس بازپسین یار شوی

Tell the night it cannot claim our day –
In love's religion there are no rules.
Love's an ocean, vast and without shores.
When lovers drown, they don't cry out or pray.

با شب می گو که روز ما را شب نیست   در مذهب عشق و عشق را مذهب نیست

عشق آن بحری ست کش کران و لب نیست   بس غرقه شوند و ناله و یا رب نیست

The harvest of my pain was its own remedy.
Low as I was, I rose to faith from heresy.
Body, heart, and soul obscured the path, until
Body melted into heart, heart in soul, soul in love itself.

تا حاصل دردم سبب درمان گشت   پستیم بلندی شد و کفر ایمان گشت
جان و دل و تن حجاب ره بود کنون   تن دل شد و دل جان شد و جان جانان گشت

Love gallops naked, off to the plains —
My heart knows him by his proud stance and feint.
It tells me, "When I too escape from form,
I will play the game of love with love's shape."

آن عشق مجرد سوی صحرا می تاخت   دیدش دل من ز کرو فرش بشناخت
با خود می گفت چون ز صورت برهم   با صورت عشق عشق ها خواهم باخت

As long as I live, this is my work, my trade,
My calm, my peace, my companion in grief.
I'm no hunter but I live to stalk this prey.
This is what fills my day, my destiny.

تا من بزیم پیشه و کارم اینست صیادنیم صید و شکارم اینست

روزم اینست و روزگارم اینست آرام و قرار و غمگسارم اینست

The dew of love turned man's dust to clay,
From which grew unruly passion's horde.
Their hundred spears pierced the veins of soul.
What we call heart is one drop of its blood.

از شبنم عشق خاک آدم گل شد صد فتنه و شور در جهان حاصل شد

صد نشتر عشق بر رگ روح زدند یک قطره از آن چکید و نامش دل شد

You are water, we are all plants that drink.
We are all beggars, you are the king.
We are all voices, you're the one who speaks.
Why don't we follow? You're the one who seeks.

تو آبی و ما جمله گیاهیم همه   تو شاهی و ما جمله گداییم همه

گویند تویی و ما صداییم همه   جوینده تویی چرا نیاییم همه

The king who pleaded mercy for all sins has gone —
Gone the night more lovely than a thousand moons.
If he returns and finds me not, then say,
"Like you who just pass through, he's gone away."

شاهی که شفیع هر گنه بود برفت   وانشب که به از هزار مه بود برفت

گر باز آید مرا نبیند تو بگوی   او نیز چو تو بر سر ره بود برفت

What is sadness, that lays siege to the hearts
Of men who are withered, cold, and bitter?
The heart that holds God holds an ocean,
Whose joyous waves make the earth turn.

غم کیست که گرد دل مردان گردد   غم گرد فسردگان و سردان گردد

اندر دل مردان خدا دریاییست   کز موج خوشش کنبد گردان گردد

I am lost in God, and God in me.
Why look in all directions? Look within.
I am the Lord — I would wrong you to say
That anyone is Lord or God to me.

من محو خدایم و خدا آن منست   هر سویش مجویید که در جان منست

سلطان منم و غلط نایم به شما   گویم که کسی هست که سلطان منست

When you remind me of the night before,
I feel the rapture surging up once more.
How can I forget that blessing ever,
When you bring to my mind buried treasure?

ای آن که تو از دوش بیادم دادی   زان حالت پرجوش بیادم دادی

آن رحمت را کجا فراموش کنم   کز گنج فراموش بیادم دادی

The scent of you will never leave my nose.
The vision of your face won't leave my eyes.
A lifetime long I've dreamt you, night and day.
That life has passed but the dream remains.

هرگز ز دماغ بنده بوی تو نرفت   وز دیده من خیال روی تو نرفت

در آرزوی تو عمر بردم شب و روز   عمرم همه رفت و آرزوی تو نرفت

You're sitting beside the road that you seek.
Blinded by moonlight, you search for the moon.
Why seek Joseph's beauty, his dimpled chin?
You yourself are Joseph, you are him. [8]

ای بر سرِ ره نشسته ره میطلبی   در خرمن مه فتاده مه میطلبی

در چاه زنخدان چنین یوسف حسن   خود دلو توئی یوسف و چه میطلبی

They say love means crying out her name — lies!
They say love's hope will never ripen — lies!
A universe of joy lives within us.
They say it lies beyond the sky — all lies!

گویند که عشق بانک نا ست دروغ   گویند امید عشق خواست دروغ

کیوان سعادت بر مادر جانست   گویند فراز هفت با ست دروغ

Absolute joy has no room for sadness,
Nor has the heart that rests beyond the sky.
He whose mind dwells in the hanging stars
Will not sow seeds of sadness on this earth.

کی غم خورد آن که شاد مطلق باشد   و آن دل که برون ز چرخ ازرق باشد
تخم غم را کجا پذیرد بزمین   آن کز هوسش فلک معلق باشد

When mankind gathers on that final day,
And faces pale from fear of reckoning,
I'll hold your love in the palm of my hand,
And I will say, "By this I'm saved or damned."

فردا که بمحشر اندر آید زن و مرد   از یم حساب روی ها گردد زرد
من عشق ترا بکف نهم پیش برم   گویم که حساب من از این باید کرد

Like friends united, it's a season blessed.
Heart's light is sparked to life by body's death.
At the sound of lightning laughing, clouds cry.
The garden laughs as tears fall from the sky.

فصلیست چو وصل دوست فرخنده شده   از مردن تن چراغ دل زنده شده
از خنده برق ابر در گریه شده   وز گریه ابر باغ در خنده شده

Eternal, beginningless love made you sing,
Love bedazzled and made a fool of you.
You died of longing — your reward was life.
What you so yearned for, finally you became.

از عشق ازل ترانه گویان گشتی   وز حیرت عشق گول و نادان گشتی
از بسکه بمردی ز غمش جان بردی   وز بسکه بگفتی غم آن آن گشتی

Love holds all Eastern alchemy,
A cloud that hides a thousand thunderbolts.
Inside me its glory fills an ocean,
A universe where all creation drowns.

عشقست که کیمیای شرقست در او   ابریست که صد هزار برقست در او

در باطن من ز فر او دریاییست   کاین جمله کاینات غرقست در او

The turning sky conceals in its heart
Sweet secrets we once spoke together,
But one day will spill them like raindrops cast wide,
And our words will bloom across the world.

آن خوش سخنان که ما بگفتیم بهم   در دل دارد نهفته این چرخ به خم

یک روز چو باران کند او غمازی   بر روید سر ما ز صحن عالم

Moonlight Brings, Moonlight Takes Away

مهتاب بدادو باز مهتاب ببرد

TO IRANIANS, RUMI is known simply as MOLANA — "our master"— a title that honors his greatness as a teacher. His masterpiece is a vast ocean of a poem called the MASNAVI, a collection of teaching stories in 25,000 verses, written during the last years of his life. But even in many of these very brief poems from the DIVAN-E SHAMS, we hear the teacher's voice.

There are echoes here of ancient, pre-Islamic tradition, for the earliest known rubaiyat are gnomic Zoroastrian poems offering maxims to live by. Many of Rumi's aphorisms have another familiar flavor, almost perfect expressions of Buddhist themes: impermanence, equanimity, and the illusory nature of existence. These echoes may seem less startling if we remember that Rumi's birthplace, Balkh, was an important center of both Zoroastrian religion and Buddhism, as well as an outpost of the Greek empire.

However bold he was in declaring the common ground of all faiths — the heartland of the "religion of love" that he explored fearlessly — and merciless in lambasting pious hypocrisy, Rumi lived his life as teacher of Islam and its mystical tradition.

The messenger brings sad news,
But words cannot obscure the truth:
Write "prison" on the garden gate —
That word does not a prison make.

قاصدی پی اینکه بنده خندان نشود پنهان مکن از بنده که پنهان نشود

گر بر در باغی بنویسی زندان باغ از پی آن نوشته زندان نشود

My turban, my cloak, and my head —
All three are worth less than a cent.
My name is not heard in the world.
I'm nobody, nobody, nobody.

دستار سر و جبه من هر سه به هم قیمت کردندـه به یک درم چیزی کم

نشنیده‌ستی تو نام من در عالم من هیچ کم هیچ کم هیچ کم

A dervish needs to know pain's presence,
Needs to know himself, alone in its midst.
Again, they build another monastery.
All earth's a monastery — it only needs true men.

درویشی را بنقد دردی باید · وانگه ز میان درد فردی باید

ز هر طرف از صومعه‌ای ساخته‌اند · عالم همه صومعه است مردی باید

The simpler our hands and hearts, the more free
Of the world around, the happier we'll be.
Penniless pleasure, gone in a blink,
Is better than the pomp of a thousand kings.

دست و دل ما هر چه تهی تر خوش تر · و آزادی دل ز هر چه در بر خوش تر

عیش خوش مفلسانه یک چشم زدن · از حشمت صد هزار قیصر خوشتر

Yesterday, fortune lit up our day.
Today the world's consumed by burning flames.
A pity that in my life's book, God's hand
Wrote, "That was one day, this too just one day."

دی بود چنان دولت و جان افروزی و امروز چنین آتش عالم سوزی

افسوس که در دفتر ما دست خدا آن را روزی نبشت این را روزی

I'm content with this way: nonexistence.
Why so much advice about existence?
The day I die by that blade, Non-being,
I will laugh at whoever cries for me.

زینگونه که من به نیستی خرسندم چندین چه دهید بهر هستی پندم

روزی که به تیغ نیستی بکشدم گرینده من کیست بر او می خندم

Seek the wisdom that unties for you this knot.
Seek the way forward that takes your whole life.
Leave that nothing that looks like it's something,
Seek the thing that looks like nothing — it's not.

علمی که ترا گره گشاید بطلب   زان پیش که از تو جان برآید بطلب

آن نیست که هست مینماید بگذار   آن هست که نیست مینماید بطلب

A few flies are brawling over sugar
Like it's treasure. Why should the sugar care?
A bird lands on the mountain, flies again.
Is the mountain bigger or smaller then?

بر کان شکر چند مگس را غوغاست   کی کان شکر را بمگس ها پرواست

مرغی که بر آن کوه نشست و برخاست   بنگر که بر آن کوه چه افزود و چه کاست

All souls alive have souls — soul itself does not.
There's bread for all the hungry — what feeds bread?
Any good thing in the world you can think of
Is subject to change, except life's source itself.

جان هاست همه جانوران را جز جان   نان هاست همه نان طلبان را جز نان

هر چیز خوشی که در جهان فرض کنی   آن را بدل و عوض بود جز جانان

Love makes you thirst? Never fear, you have wine.
Your waters run dry? No, there's water nearby.
Your body's a ruin? There's treasure inside!
Wake up! This world you dream is nothing to fear.

مرتشهٔ عشق را شرابیست مترس   بی آب شدی پیش تو آبیست مترس

گنجی تو اگر تنت خرابیست مترس   بیدار شو از جهان که خوابیست مترس

Those who flow like water, clear and clean,
Flow like wine in us through mind and vein.
I stretched myself out and humbly lay down,
Like a boat for men to ride this stream.

آن ها که چو آب صافی و ساده روند   اندر رگ و مغز چون می و باده روند
من پای کشیدم و دراز افتادم   اندر کشتی دراز و افتاده روند

If you walk with eyes shut, you'll lose your way.
But lean on sight and you unleash destruction.
Don't look within the monastery or mosque
To find a place that has no location.

بی دیده اگر راه روی عین خطاست   بر دیده اگر تکیه زدی تیر بلاست
در صومعه و مدرسه از راه مجاز   آنراکه نه جا است تو چه دانی کجاست؟

The friend to whom rose and thorn are one,
In whose faith Cross and Koran are the same –
Why should I worry? To him it's all one –
Lame donkey, swift horse, all the same.

در مذہب او مصحف و زنار یکیست   یاری که بنزد او گل و خار یکیست

کو را خر لنگ و اسب رہوار یکیست   ما را غم آن یار چرا باید خورد

At times we are hidden, at times revealed.
We are Muslims, Christians, Jews, of any race.
Until our hearts are shaped to hold all hearts,
We show these different faces to the world.

که مومن و که یہود و که ترسائیم   مائیم که گه نہان و که پیدائیم

ہر روز به صورتی برون می آئیم   تا این دل ما قالب ہر دل گردد

You do bad and hope to get back good,
Though in return bad only gives back bad.
Though God may be merciful and kind,
If you plant barley, wheat won't grow.

بد می کنی و نیک طمع می داری   هم بد باشد سزای بد کرداری

با اینکه خداوند کریم است و رحیم   گندم ندمد بار چو جو می کاری

You are all held captive behind this veil,
But if you escape you will yet be kings.
Life's waters speak to all creatures, "Die!
All of you, die on the shore of my stream!"

هر چند در این پرده اسیرید همه   زین پرده برون روید امیرید همه

آن آب حیات خلق را می گوید   بر ساحل جوی ما بمیرید همه

Choose only drunks and lovers to commune with,
Don't be lured into low company.
Each tribe pulls you into its own circle –
The parrot sings of sugar, of ruins, the crow.

جز صحبت عاشقان و مستان مپسند   دل در هوس قوم فرومایه مبند

هر طایفه ات بجانب خویش کشند   زاغت سوی ویرانه و طوطی سوی قند

Hide other's faults deep in the earth
If their actions make you feel shame.
If you mirror both their good and bad
Then you yourself must be polished steel.

گر شرم همی از آن و این باید داشت   پس عیب کسان زیر زمین باید داشت

ور آینه وار نیک و بد بنمائی   چون آینه روی آهنین باید داشت

You're so coupled to life, which lasts a day,
That you can't even hear talk of death.
Life looks for a home and that home is death,
But your donkey fell asleep on the way.

با جان دو روزه تو چنان گشتی جفت   با تو سخن مرگ نمی شاید گفت

جان طالب منزلست و منزل مرگست   اما خر تو میانهٔ راه بخفت

Hatred, greed, jealousy — toss them from your heart.
Suspicion and bad habits — reform them.
Deny this and you lose — cut your losses.
Own this and your profits quickly grow.

حرص و حسد و کینه ز دل بیرون کن   خوی بد و اندیشه تو دیگرگون کن

انکار زیان تست، زو کمتر گیر   اقرار ترا سود دهد، افزون کن

None of these stone hearts have softened yet,
Not one of the frozen has ever warmed.
Your tanner hasn't started – this hide is raw.
No one here has yet been struck by your awe.

زین سنگدلان نشد دلی نرم هنوز   زین یخ صفتان یکی نشد گرم هنوز

نگرفت دباغت آخر این چرم هنوز   نگرفت یکی راز خدا شرم هنوز

Time will soon silence these bleating sheep,
The wolf of doom will devour the flock.
Each of their heads is stuffed with pride,
Death's slap on the neck will knock it out.

کوتاه کند زمانه این دم دمه را   وز هم بدرد گرگ فنا این رمه را

اندر سر هر کسی غروریست ولی   سیلی اجل قفا زند این همه را

Looking outside, you see lifeless faces,
Strangers all, from Rome to Khorasan.
"Come home," He commanded. "Look within
To see what is not human but divine."

بیرون نگری صورت بی جان بینی   خلقی عجب از روم و خراسان بینی

فرمود که ارجعی رجوع آن باشد   بنگر به درون که بجز انسان بینی

The tides will take my poetry and song,
And carry off the clothes I did not own.
Good and bad, devotion, empty piety —
Moonlight brings and moonlight takes away.

بیت و غزل و شعر مرا آب ببرد   رختی که نداشتیم سیلاب ببرد

نیک و بد زهد و پارسایی را   مهتاب بداد و باز مهتاب ببرد

Endnotes

1. Scholars have mapped a maze of variations in different manuscripts. The reader is referred to Ibrahim Gamard and Rawan Farhadi, *The Quatrains of Rumi*, San Rafael, California: Sufi Dari Books, 2008, for an overview in English and notes on the individual quatrains. The poems for these translations were drawn, with a few exceptions, from the one-volume Forouzanfar edition based on the incomplete 1941 Isfahan edition. As such, they reflect a popular selection familiar to non-specialist Iranian readers today, rather than the most accurate scholarship currently available.

2. *Maqâlât-e Shams-e Tabrizi*, quoted in Franklin D. Lewis, *Rumi - Past and Present, East and West. The Life, Teachings, and Poetry of Jalâl al-Din Rumi*, Oxford: Oneworld Publications, (UK), 2000. p. 153

3. Mansour Al-Hallaj was a Sufi saint who was executed in 922 in Baghdad for proclaiming "I am the Truth," which was seen as a blasphemous claim to divinity, but understood by Sufis as spoken from a state of unification with the divine.

4. *Maqâlât-e Shams-e Tabrizi*, quoted in Franklin D. Lewis, *Rumi - Past and Present, East and West: The Life, Teachings,*

and Poetry of Jalâl al-Din Rumi, Oxford: Oneworld Publications, (UK), 2000. p. 182

5   Majnoon wandered the desert, driven insane by separation from his beloved Leyla.

6   Khotan was an ancient Buddhist kingdom and an important oasis on the Silk Road, renowned in Rumi's time for the beauty of its inhabitants.

7   I have taken a slight liberty with this verse. I've used "Mecca" instead of the original KA'BAH, and what I've rendered as "Bodhgaya" is originally BOT-KHANEH, which means temple or, literally, "house of idols." The word BOT, which has come to mean idol in modern Persian, in earlier Persian languages referred to the Buddha.

8   The Biblical stories of Joseph also occur in the Qoran, where he is described as a paragon of beauty. In the Qoranic version of the story, Joseph's brothers push him into a well, and the well's bucket later serves for his rescue. The final line of the poem on p. 180 translates literally as, "You yourself are the bucket, why search for Joseph?"

Acknowledgments

THESE TRANSLATIONS were originally published daily, beginning in April 2000, in the online magazine *Iranian.com*. I am indebted to the editor, Jahanshah Javid, for creating the circumstances that inspired the translations and for his selection of the original verses that were my daily assignment.

Over the years, many people have helped me to improve those first efforts. I am grateful to the many online readers who offered feedback, to Farbod Rohaniyan and Abbas Daneshvari who offered expert advice on many points of interpretation, and to Robert Bly who pushed me to recalibrate my aim for the English verse.

I have relied on the work of two scholars that I would recommend to anyone interested in understanding Rumi's poetry more deeply. Franklin D. Lewis's *Rumi — Past and Present, East and West: The Life, Teachings, and Poetry of Jalâl al-Din Rumi*, is the most thorough study available of Rumi's life and the historical and literary context of his writing. The *Quatrains of Rumi* translated by Ibrahim Gamard and Rawan Farhadi is a recently published, annotated, and carefully literal translation of the quatrains that has rescued me from many a false step.

In the transition from a perpetual project to the book in hand, Amanda Tong's graceful assistance has been essential. Her keen eye and insights were especially helpful in the final selection of the verses and editing of the text. I'm thankful for guidance from Mansour Taeed and Majid Roshangar, for Colin Wright's help with the Kickstarter campaign, for the composition of the Persian text by Elham Shareghi, and for the beautiful book design by Kathleen Burch.